EARTH PONDS

EARTH PONDS

The Country Pond Maker's Guide
to Building, Maintenance and Restoration

Second Edition, Revised and Expanded

TIM MATSON

COUNTRYMAN PRESS   •   WOODSTOCK, VERMONT

Thanks To All Who Helped
Pond makers & Pond keepers Leonard Cook, Sonny Stearns, Sherm Stebbins, George Williams, Gordon Wilder, Harold and Calvin Day, Jim Malone, Steve Wetmore, Ralph Stevens, Donny Prescott, Joseph and Flo Morse, Peter Orgain, Woody Ransom, Karl Hammer, Blake and Aletta Traendly, Henry Marckes, Hank McGreevey, Bob Huke, Ray Uline, Ron Hansen and the Eastman community, Mark Lornell, David Talbot, Lila Stutz-Lumbra, Gary Ullman, Ted Kenyon, Sean Mullen, and Dr. John Dwyer.

Neighbors Eric and Cheslye Darnell, Gerard Stevens, and Vi Coffin.

Book People Peter Jennison, Chris Lloyd, and the staff of The Countryman Press, Katinka Matson and John Brockman, Guy Russell, Bob Gere, Jeffrey Nintzel, Gordon Pine, Roger Griffith, and the Sun Photographic Lab & Gallery.

Parts of *Earth Ponds* appeared in *Harrowsmith, Farmstead,* and *CoEvolution Quarterly.*

Book design by Guy Russell
Cover Design by Matt Ralph
Illustrations by Diane St. Jean
Typeset by NK Graphics
Printed by Courier
Photographs by the Author

Library of Congress Cataloging-in-Publication Data

Matson, Tim
    Earth ponds : the country pond maker's guide / Tim Matson. —Rev. and expanded ed.
    p. cm.
Includes bibliographical references and index.
ISBN 0-88150-155-7
1. Water-supply, Rural—Amateurs' manuals.   2. Ponds—Amateurs' manuals.
   I. Title.
TD927.M434 1991
627'.86—dc20   90-26957
                                                     CIP

Contents

"And like the fishponds of the abbeys and castles of medieval Europe and the Dark Ages, when all the world fell apart in anarchy and disorder, they provide not only food for the table but peace for the soul and an understanding of man's relationship to the universe."

Louis Bromfield
Malabar Farm

For Ellen Langtree

Preface to the Second Edition

Lots of water has gone over the dam in the ten years since the first edition of *Earth Ponds*. The book was written in the aftermath of the late 70s' oil crunch, in a spirit of self-sufficiency and planetary stewardship, about a subject previously confined to farmers and professional aquaculturists. Then during the 1980s, pond building caught on with the public. The economy went through an unprecedented boom, and in its wake thousands of new ponds appeared across the continent, ponds for recreation and fishing leading the way. Water gardening became one of the hottest trends in domestic landscaping, spurring interest in aquatic plants and shrubs that thrive around ponds, as well as methods for maintaining water quality. People began excavating and restoring ponds as refuges for endangered waterfowl and wildlife. Conservation of natural resources, including mandatory wetland construction to offset loss to development, became a national policy. Recently, when the economy took another dive, interest turned again to more frugal methods of pond excavation. At the same time, a combination of environmental regulations restricting pond excavation in sensitive wetland areas, and high real estate construction costs, prompted new interest in pond restoration.

The result is a more sophisticated level of interest in pond use. Hence this new edition. Originally the focus had been on pond construction: siting, design, working with contractors, and excavation; all with an emphasis on saving money by undertaking much of the preparation yourself. But there was another dimension that had been skimmed over: pond care. Gradually, over the past decade, many of the ponds that I helped design began to need maintenance and repairs, including my own. Algae, weeds, leaks, silt, and erosion, all natural signs of pond aging, began turning up. Traditional methods of pond maintenance emphasize toxic chemicals and expensive dredging. Looking for better alternatives, I began to explore aeration, biological management, and structural and hydrological improvements.

Building a pond from scratch is one thing. Reviving an old or ailing pond is another. There it sits. It may be loaded with silt or algae, or choked with weeds. It may leak. Perhaps it's empty. The pond may have been dug decades before the present owner took possession of the land, with entirely different, perhaps opposing goals in mind. Yet inside that old swimming hole is a new pond waiting to emerge, often in better shape than the original.

In the Pond Care chapter you will discover a wide spectrum of up-to-date, efficient techniques for bringing ponds back to life. For example, inexpensive flexible plastic piping makes it easier to feed ponds supplementary water, reviving structures that might have been previously abandoned or bulldozed under. Hydraulic excavators allow for quick, surgically accurate edge cleanups. PVC liners and other leak-proofing methods can be used to hold water in porous ponds. Aerators give dead waters new life, and hybrid fish gobble up intrusive weeds and algae, eliminating the need for chemicals.

Pond restoration can be tricky. In many instances, the pond should be emptied. That brings up the matter of drainage, which must be handled so that downstream areas are not damaged by flooding or silt. If a pond is to be cleaned out, partially or completely, keep in mind that the pondbed seal that helps hold water is likely to be disturbed and should be restored. Otherwise, a leak will result. Off-the-shelf leak remedies don't usually mention the tricky part: how to pinpoint exactly where the seepage occurs. Restoration techniques, including tracking down leaks, are discussed in Pond Care. For quick reference, a trouble-shooting guide to pond problems, their possible causes and solutions, is to be found in Part Three.

Choosing a method of water quality control requires thinking about not only your pond, but your downstream neighbor's water supply as well. Chemicals can be used to kill algae and weeds, but they also can kill fish and bacterial life, and may contaminate the watershed. In many cases, manual removal of intrusive plants is best. Often aeration is offered as a non-toxic panacea for everything from algae to fish kills, but there are several different types of aerators, each with a different capacity for water quality improvement. Careful selection is required to match the pond and equipment. In the Controlling Pond Weeds and Algae, and Healthy Ponds Need Plenty of Fresh Air chapters, you will learn about different plant and water quality maintenance methods, including aeration methods and applications.

Interest in pond "solutions" should not be limited to water quality and structural repairs alone. Ponds also can be used as solutions in themselves to provide refuge for endangered waterfowl and wildlife. Shallow man-made ponds can be used to offset wetland losses to development and agricultural drainage. This suggests new uses for old marshy ponds and shallow bays, until recently neglected or eliminated by designers and owners.

I often suggest to people repairing ponds that part of the shoreland be allowed to remain wild. Rather than creating a totally manicured appearance, preserving a stretch of brush and emergent vegetation will offer cover and food for wildlife. Pond owners who try this are usually rewarded with an increase in visits from waterfowl and wild critters. Wild game food nurseries offer seeds and root stock for plants especially attractive to wildlife. In Ponds for Waterfowl and Wildlife you will learn how wildlife pond design and plantings create such "solutions," and the expanded appendix lists sources of seeds and root stock.

For many pond designers and contractors, landscaping around ponds has been a thorny issue. Because of a traditional emphasis on water quality and structural integrity, plantings are often discouraged. This gets around the problem of fertilizer seepage, root damage to embankments, and foliage fallout in the basin. But it also results in a barren layout. Fortunately, the proliferation of water garden nurseries across the country has made a large variety of aquatic plants available; many require little if any fertilizer and can be managed to prevent pond intrusion. In Pondscapes, you will learn about this new approach to landscaping around water. The updated Appendix features many new sources of plants and water gardening paraphernalia.

Finally, for those who don't yet own a pond or contemplate building one, there's always the opportunity to buy one. You will have to buy the land around it as well, and perhaps a house overlooking the water. Of course, there's more to buying a pond than simply writing a check. In How to Buy a Used Pond you will find plenty of clues for selecting a good old pond. And some suggestions about selling one, for that matter.

December 1990, Strafford, Vermont

Prologue

How many historians have looked at the evolutionary link between people and ponds? Only Lewis Mumford comes close when he observes that man's manipulation of containers preceded his tool-making:

> Our present overcommitment to technics is in part due to a radical misinterpretation of the whole course of human development . . . there is still a tendency to identify tools and machines with technology . . . this practice overlooks the equally vital role of containers: first hearths, pits, traps, cordage; later baskets, bins, byres, houses, to say nothing of still later collective containers like reservoirs . . . .

I chanced across this thought one night while basking in the glow of the wood stove and a quart of home brew. A marvelous notion struck me. The "tool" with the most promise for this homestead had to be the pond on the side hill.

Mumford never sharpens his focus on ponds. Yet pond making first enabled humans to build agricultural settlements with guaranteed irrigation. And through time ponds have done it all: nurtured fish and safeguarded castles, frozen ice for food storage, and turned industrial power. The Chinese built man's most enduring civilization on a foundation of ponds. The revolutionary United States gained independence with the help of ponds that drove mills to produce cider, flour, feed, lumber, and textiles. In fact, life on earth began in a shallow sunlit pond. A single-celled organism with the miraculous ability to reproduce woke up one warm day and has been evolving ever since.

The first deliberate impoundment of water was likely a dammed pond built by beavers big as bears. These creatures changed the planet. Their ponds nursed new plant and animal life, filled subterranean springs, and silted into fertile valley lands. Somebody was watching. In primeval Europe and Scandinavia "lake dwellers" began to build pole houses over water. Climbing ahead of their cave-dwelling kin on the evolutionary ladder, these reformed nomads worked together cutting and trimming trees and floating timbers out to their off-shore building sites. Anchored there amid food and water they lived secure from interlopers. Academics consider the lake dwellers a turning point in human development. They miss seeing that the first lake dwellers were simply aping their neighbors, a colony of beavers.

The Egyptians, who clearly knew the beaver since they depicted its exploits in hieroglyphics, were among the first to practice irrigation; they held water from the spring Nile behind dams for release during drought. About the same time, in beaver-inhabited China, rice growers learned to dam streams to create fertile paddies. Did beavers inspire those dams and fish ponds? Ask a North American Cherokee. In his cosmology it was a beaver that mated with the Great Spirit, transforming the hostile elements into rich earth.

As late as 1700 a pond civilization of more than 100 million beavers inhabited North America. Streams supported beaver colonies in close succession, as many as 300 to the mile. At Three Forks, Montana, in 1805, Lewis and Clark looked out over beaver ponds stretching to the horizon. Settlers used water from beaver ponds to power the first mills, and clearings around ponds made inviting village sites. Silted ponds became rich meadows for grazing cattle, and beaver dams tempered floods and reserved water during drought.

But beaver hides grew more valued than ponds. Pelts traded with Europeans brought vast sums of money, feeding financial empires like the Astors' and the Hudson Bay Company. *Castoreum*—beaver oil—found an eager market in Europe as a perfume and stimulant. White men and native Americans plundered the wilderness, trapping beaver year round, and by the end of the nineteenth century the species was close to extinction.

In this century the beaver has been nursed back, but not for its fur or its oil. The beaver is back to build ponds. In New Hampshire, where beaver trapping is carefully regulated, state game superintendent Henry Laramie told the *New Hampshire Times,* "The beaver has probably done more for waterfowl management and other species than anything else in one-hundred years." In western states beavers are dropped by parachute into national forests to reestablish oases of wildlife in clearcut timberland and to provide buffers against erosion and forest fire. Beaver ponds in Maine are the last refuges of the rare blueback trout. In Mississippi, state wildlife specialists are nurturing a growing duck population by sowing millet in the state's 24,000 acres of beaver ponds.

If beavers lured men into pond making, they offered no guarantees. Their technique of damming streams is the most difficult pond-making style. In fact, given a suitable pond in a secure neighborhood, a beaver colony will forego pond making completely and build instead a dwelling lodge with canals for food and timber transport. Where nature has skimped on ponds, beavers dam a body of water deep enough to protect a lodge entrance, prevent freezing of underwater food supplies, and fill transportation canals. If beavers are already established, a simple barrier of saplings and mud is often enough to add a new pond to a stream or headwater. But in virgin terrain it may take the labor of several generations to develop a thriving colony.

After selecting a pond site, the beavers begin gnawing down trees, pushing and floating their lumber to the dam. Contrary to myth, beavers do not build dams by felling trees cross-stream. They layer green saplings parallel with the waterflow, freshly chewed butts upstream about a foot higher than crowns. As the barrier rises, the weight of the dam and the pressure of the current hook the timbers into the stream bed, like anchors. In a swift stream beavers weigh trees in place with stones and mud. The layered poles knit together and reinforce the bracing. Beavers like young green deciduous saplings best, about five inches at the stump. After some good chewing and a warning thump of the tail, the critter scrambles away, and the tree drops. If the crown tangles and the tree hangs up, the beaver may try again. But the animal is not immune to logging's deadly risks, and he knows it; after a couple of unsuccessful attempts to loosen the snag, the beaver will usually leave the tree hanging.

Where no saplings grow, beavers improvise. "Grass beavers" use cobblestones or chunks of coal gathered from cliffs. Logjam dams are put together from timbers rolled and skidded downhill over snow. After a forest fire, beavers use the charred trees for the dam and reserve undamaged groves for food.

As the pond begins to fill, water streaming through the dam plugs the chinks with sediment and brush, and the dam waterproofs itself. If the dam won't hold enough water, the beavers plaster it with mud and grass roots. When the water level reaches an agreeable point, the beavers arrange to maintain it. In some ponds this means keeping a loose dam that seeps water through the structure; in others, a waterfall carries the spill. The most successful beavers build spillways that guide the overflow away from the dam, so not to undermine it.

The pond doesn't always work. A colony may begin a dam near an insufficient timber stand or overestimate the water supply. For a remedy, the beavers might try digging new canals to bring in extra water or timber to heighten the dam. Or they might excavate another foot or two throughout the basin. If the pond still looks too shallow, the colony will scout for a new site and move on.

The lesson of the beaver pond is simple. Natural ponds refuse to seal perfectly, and success is never guaranteed. Beaver ponds evolve non-stop as the animals touch up leaks, channel water, and raise the dam to keep up with incoming sediment. If spring rains and snowmelt blow out the dam, the beavers will build another. Beavers thrive on fixing ponds. Who wouldn't, with webbed hind feet, waterproof fur, and teeth that never quit growing?

I discovered the art of pond culture by a fluke. A decade ago I was on the lookout for a small farm in Orange County, Vermont, in cahoots with my sweetheart, who had joined me packing for the hills. On one rickety farm we found an old earth pond. I wasn't able to get near it because I was on crutches after a skiing crack-up, and Diana couldn't see much under three feet of snow. But I figured the pond would provide good therapy for my leg, and she was half-fish at least. So we handed over our savings.

My cast came off after the snowmelt in the spring, and I felt strong enough for swimming. Alas, I found the pond in need of restoration. It had dehydrated; the sidepipe that fed it stream water was clogged. So over the next couple of years I tended the pond and swam my leg back into shape. I reestablished the smooth flow of stream water, cleared the plugged spillway, hauled silt from the delta where water entered the basin, and stocked the pond with rainbow trout. I set up a gravity-feed watering hose from the pond downhill to the barn and garden, and for Christmas I built a redwood sauna close to the shore to enable us to stretch the swimming season full-length between thaw and freeze. That was the beginning of my romance with ponds.

Naturally, according to the law of thermodynamics, something had to give. It turned out to be Diana. We sold the farm, split up the trout, and rambled off to chase our different fates.

Now, fifteen years down the road, I live in a homemade cabin overlooking a quarter-acre apple-green pond that I sited, cleared, and carved in collaboration with a bulldozer sculptor. Happily, not long ago I hooked up with a mountain mermaid. Together we cultivate most of our own food and collect all our firewood and lumber, with some surplus left over to barter with neighbors in the hills. Seventy-five trout fatten in the pond, and surplus water gravity-feeds a rich market garden and a winter pig. Long range pond schemes include a firefighters' pump, a small hydro generator, a wood-fired sauna, and an ice house. Our holding will swell with pond power.

Beyond this I've found a new dimension in the pleasures of pond making. Of all the bucolic arts and husbandries, pond making alone seems to balance the forces that animate the land—nature and man. You can carve a pond and step back, as people have done since the beginning of history, and the pond comes alive. More than a thousand years ago the Chinese poet Han Yu wrote:

Does the bowl
in the garden
mock nature
when night after night
green frogs gather
to prove it's a pool?
Who says
you can't make a pond
out of a bowl?

Pond making was a sacred Eastern tradition. Monks carved ponds beside their temples and shrines to mirror the universe. These shining objects of concentration distilled the Buddha's message. Reflected in the water the moon was pure illusion, empty form. There was nothing to discover but the nature of mind. In the West, pond making was first celebrated in 1559 when Janus Dubravius, Bishop of Bohemia, published *A New Booke of Good Husbandry*. His intention was to reveal "the secret commodities in making fish ponds, and furnishing the same." Yet despite all the practical advantages of earth ponds, Dubravius had to confess, "In our country of ponds . . . it may appear that fish with their ponds were instruments more to feed the eyes than for sustenance or food." Thoreau's *Walden* was a later tribute to ponds as objects of contemplation.

If earth ponds stimulate such rich visions—and harvests—can't pond making be seen as an art? (A little Buddhist simplicity wouldn't hurt a bit either.) I didn't appreciate this until I had built my own pond and labored on several others. Then, after watching three ponds empty through faulty spillway piping, and comparing my $850 reservoir with half a dozen $6,000 ponds of similar capacity, I could see why the rate of contemporary pond making was not rising along with the opportunities for low-cost aquaculture.

An aesthetic independence is needed to balance the super-pond mentality of many engineers and contractors. Otherwise, too many new, overpriced ponds will wind up in unnatural sites with earth embankments sticking up like sore thumbs, pierced with superfluous piping dripping inside and out.

I have a thriftier vision: a patchwork sea of homemade pond sculptures across the land.

14

Part I
The Cabin Pond

Digging In

Flood

On Ice

Spring

Scouts

Flow to the Garden

Bishop of Ponds

Predators and Prey

Blending In

Digging In

Conceived by a 15-ton Caterpillar one warm June morning, the new pond grew slowly through the summer drought, swelling with the juice of invisible springs. Luck was with me. All around, the Green Mountains were turning brown and the corn stood still. By July, my well, like others nearby, had dried up. From the hill I watched my neighbors drive to the village with jugs for water. When the wind blew, their gardens grew dust. In the early mornings all through the drought I skimmed off clear bucketsful of water for the day's cooking and washing. Then I dove in, stirring up clouds of mud—which bothered me not at all. After my mineral bath I lay in the sunrise to dry while the pond steamed like a giant cappucino. Still later, after irrigating the garden, I brewed coffee for myself. Same water. It was a good year to carve a pond.

Instinct led me to water. Hill life is incomplete without access to a brook or a pond. My shallow spring supplied me well, but my spirit was tinder. I could build a cabin with a chain saw and thrive without electricity, but the cracker-dry sidehill made me chafe. So did the oily outboards in the nearby lake. In early spring I began planning the pond. A likely site lay a stone's throw downhill from the cabin, an acre of alder swamp bubbling with underground springs and fed by an overland vein of mountain water. To be sure, I called on the free counsel of the local conservation agent, who came out and bored into the muck with his auger and pulled out an encouraging amount of watertight clay. He suggested that I dig test holes to gauge soil depth and water supply. In the fall I hired a backhoe cowboy to dig a well, and while he was here I asked him to scoop out two test holes at the site where I envisioned the pond. These pockets filled fast and held water. So when the sun rolled around again in the spring, I started to clear the land.

So far my pond investment had come to about ten dollars in backhoe time and fifty cents in phone calls. Clearing the swamp added little to the list of expenses, but it turned into the toughest effort of the whole endeavor. Armed with a smoking McCulloch 10-10 chain saw, I slogged through a steaming jungle of thick alder, puncturing my boots on glistening stumps and sinking up to my knees in muck. Gradually I discovered a peculiar rhythm in swamp clearing. Plunging deep in mud from tree to tree sapped my strength, but then cutting didn't require much effort; having sunk down to eye level with the base of the tree, I could saw it off at the roots without even bending over. And, despite a full dressing of spring foliage, the alder was light enough to wing over my shoulder into the brush heaps ringed around the site. No dragging heavy timbers through the muck.

A neighbor warned me that bulldozing the debris under is a poor strategy, at best. Rotting organic matter can unplug the best-planned pond.

"She'll leak," he said.

To avoid leaving pockets of brush that would rot, collapse, and lead to the downfall of the pond, I gathered the dead branches and waste wood into piles. These were kept small to dry quickly and burn safely.

And so the pond clearing bloomed in tune with the undulations of backwoods inspiration. In other words, I took my time. In that spirit, I cleared the swamp by Halloween.

A white tide swept into the mountains, and the cabin seemed to float in an ocean of snow. At night by the light of a kerosene lamp I sketched imaginary swimming holes and warmed the journey to spring with dreams of sun-drenched swims in my own pond. Slowly the sun came crawling back, with toasty days sandwiched between frost-bitten nights.

Spring traditionally is the season to do anything but build a pond. Bulldozers tend to disappear in the mire. The traction is poor for both excavation and the fine dressing of embankments. Yet late in May the unseasonably dry weather was on my side. I wanted to try it.

I called the agent who had taken the clay tests and asked him to check the site again. He came, eyed the water holes, and guessed it was fit. Of course, it was just a guess. If I wanted "official" Soil Conservation Service collaboration, their office would evaluate contour maps of the watershed above the pond site and blueprint an excavation and piping plan. All for free. But in exchange I would pay construction costs and agree to follow the government's directions explicitly.

"No shortcuts," said the conservation officer.

With an ex-draftee's wariness of Uncle Sam, I put that plan on hold and went out looking for a man with a bull-dozer and good grades in pond construction.

Down in the valley lived a friend who had recently put in an elegant pond. Swimming there a year before I had marveled at the clear water, bright green banks, and gangs of rubbery tadpoles all flourishing in a pond less than a year old. I telephoned him and got the name of his pond builder.

"Hey, by the way," he blurted. "The pond dried up. It's gone."

Built in the fall, his pond filled, froze, and topped off perfectly the next spring. Then, in July, it started to leak. In a few weeks its water level was down six feet. Desperate, my friend poured in a batch of chemical sealant ominously called SS-13. This served only to pollute what remained: a crater-sized mud puddle not even suitable for ducks.

"Dragon vomit," my pal called it.

"Did you talk to the Soil Conservation Service?"

"Nope."

"Test holes?"

"Nope."

I hung up with a sinking feeling. Building ponds was for gamblers. My friend had picked up a bad hand—not enough clay in the subsoil, not enough water, not enough savvy. I had heard of other losses. But I reckoned that I had one strong card: a steadily flowing spring. Still, I grew wary. Imagine a defoliated crater in your meadow.

Nervously, I called my friend's pond builder. He arrived one bright May day, and we tramped all over the pond site. He didn't say much, except that he had four ponds in his own backyard. We trucked down into the valley so he could look back up at the mountain watershed. It reminded him of the place where he had built a six-acre giant that blew its dam and washed out the neighbors. I took a deep breath and asked him to estimate the price.

"Three thousand dollars."

He must have seen me wince.

"Or put your pond closer to the cabin. That's what I'd do. Smaller, for just two thousand."

It looked to me as if a pond close to my cabin would go dry, or float me away some dark and stormy night.

The pond maker itemized vast amounts of dirt, dams, trucking, and piping. On top of it all, he wanted to rebuild my driveway. It added up to much more money than I had imagined. Whatever became of the old-time farm pond? I wondered, as he drove off in his truck.

A couple of days later I visited my neighbors across the valley, a white-haired old couple who tend a farm and a 1,000-bucket maple sugarbush. From my desk I can see their cattle grazing and two immense gardens with a family cemetery in between. In times past they had owned my land. Down to sixty acres now, they contented themselves with a trim homestead, pond included. I told Ralph about my encounter with the pond maker. He laughed and said that he had hired a dozer and driver to dig his pond for only $200.

"That was a few years back, mind you."

He said that he knew the marsh where I planned to dig. He had watched it through scores of seasons.

"Should make a fine pond. Thought of it myself."

He recommended a good neighborhood contractor.

Walking home I felt a spatter of rain and sensed a fine afternoon for torching brush. At the edge of the marsh I found a nest holding the shells of hatched woodcock eggs. Good omen.

The brush piles flared. A fireball burst into the spring shower, scorched a birch tree fifty feet away, and sent crimson rainbows shooting through the air. When the smoke cleared, the pond was ready for excavation.

I phoned the neighborhood contractor, and a few days later he drove up in a Cadillac. While we walked over the blackened earth discussing ponds, his wife sat in the car. I've seen that before: the spiffy auto with a dutiful spouse inside. It's a sign of the reliable old-time Yankee builder. I trusted him. Besides, no one who's really making a living driving rough-riding machines goes around in a truck.

The contractor wanted to begin straightaway while the dry weather held. He estimated one or two days of primary digging, as long as the D-6 didn't sink in the swamp. Later, once the excavated earth had dried, a smaller dozer would dress the embankments. At $35 an hour, he figured on bringing in the pond for about $900.

The pond would be roughly oval in shape, with excavated earth used to build the embankment on the downhill side. No piping would be needed, we agreed. I wanted to try a natural overground spillway, eliminating the need for expensive pond plumbing to carry away excess water. It would be up to me to line the spillway with rocks to prevent erosion. Later, if the overflow began to cut away at the dam, a concrete trench could be built. He cautioned against using a horizontal pipe set at the high-water level to draw off the overflow.

"Water sneaks under there, winter comes along, and it freezes and lifts up the pipe. Then you're right back where you started."

A bottom pipe allowing complete draining of the pond would be unnecessary in this case, he felt. For an additional $500, I considered it unthrifty, to boot.

A roaring bulldozer woke me the next day. Clanking off its trailer and thundering up the hill, the yellow Caterpillar arrived like an earthquake, pumping shock waves through the ground and adrenaline into my veins. Driving the machine was a member of the contractor's dozer team. He trailed a double track of mutilated earth wherever he moved. After maneuvering the Cat into position on the uphill end of the swamp, he paused.

I greeted him, shouting over the roar of the diesel. His name was Sonny. He jumped down and tested his footing on the site, climbed back into the seat, looked at his watch, and started. Later he told me that when he stepped onto that mushy ground he felt sure the dozer would bury itself.

As it turned out, Sonny dug a beautiful pond, eight feet

deep in the middle, with no holdups. At one point we saw that the pond wanted to sidetrack into the woods. My chain saw was sharp and well-behaved, which was fortunate because water was filling in fast and Sonny had hit the point of no return. He didn't hesitate a second, smashing through the swamp, brushing past me as I dropped a slew of balsams and cut logs light enough to throw clear.

The transformation from swamp to pond was astounding. After the initial excavation, the pond filled slowly and the embankment dried. Two weeks later Sonny was back for a day with a smaller dozer to tidy up the shore. Then I raked stones out of the earth and piled them near the spillway trench. I seeded the ground with perennial rye grass, and it grew courageously despite the lack of topsoil. Except for minimal mulching I let the grass fight for itself. Fertilizer shedding into the pond would feed algae blooms, not at all conducive to a trout's health.

At the end of a month the pond was five feet deep and quit filling because of the drought. Then September rains brought in new life. The water began to rise. Later in the month, less than four months after excavation, a northeaster blew the leaves off the trees and filled the pond. I had been waiting to find the precise path the spillway would take before laying in the stones. Now, with the pond gushing over, I stood in the drenching rain and watched the water cut the trench. I let out a cheer. I didn't quit until the last rock tumbled into the spillway.

Flood

The day after the pond filled the recoil hit. The storm that had launched the pond kept up. From the cabin I watched the rain rake the water. Then I ducked into a poncho and sloshed down to the dam. The spring that usually fed the pond was flooding like a May brook. I walked around the dam. Whiskers of rye grass poked up through the embankment. In the dozer tracks grass sprouted underwater. Underfoot the earth gushed like a sponge. I followed the spillway away from the pond, checking the embankment. Turning back, I began to climb the dam. That's when the recoil hit: the pond was boiling at the rim. I backpedaled down the dam and climbed again. My heart was slamming. Making my fist a transit, I sighted the height of the dam over the water: no better than a foot and sinking. Then the crest—and the valley. It looked sure the pond would breach.

For another day the mountains squalled. A lighthouse keeper would have felt right at home in the cabin. Without a step I had moved into a watchtower. But the dam held. One November night the full moon waxed over the basin, mooring it under ice. I had all winter to worry if I had carved a teacup under a waterfall.

"Here you go."

Henry Marckes slid a pair of photographs under the stereoscope, and I looked through the glass. It was blurred gray.

"Bring the pictures together so they match along the middle edge."

I fit the images at the center. Instantly I was plucked a thousand feet into the air. Below, a mountain loomed in black and white 3-D.

"This is my land?"

"And some. That's close to a square mile."

Hardwood and evergreen saddled the mountain. Evergreens on the west slope, rock ridge for backbone, and broad-leafs on the east. But no cabin, no clearing, no pond. These photographs had been shot ahead of my time. I let my eyes roam the land.

"I'm living under a volcano."

"That's one steep watershed."

Marckes is a doctor of watersheds. With his stereoscope and a cabinet full of aerial shots, he swoops over the mountains to diagnose pond sites. I had called on him at the Randolph office of the Soil Conservation Service.

"Your site is catching runoff from about 10 acres," he calculated.

It's all one forest from a thousand feet. I didn't recognize the land. Then I spotted the four corners below my road, and Marckes pointed to a tear shape he had penciled around the pond site. It wasn't hard to conjure up a wave of runoff gathering along the ridge, spilling down the mountain through the draw that folds across the slope, and finally pouring into the pond basin.

A hundred years ago the ancestor of his 3-D viewer was called a stereophantascope. It resembled a pair of aviator goggles made of laminated wood and glass with a prop out front to stage the scenery. I once bought one, along with a shoebox full of pictures. Each view card showed two images

of the same scene photographed simultaneously through the twin lenses of a stereo camera. Since each lens caught a slightly different perspective, the viewer experienced 3-D sensations: Salvation Army nurses posed in stiff collars, Belgian horses drawing sawlogs over snow, the town stagecoach hitched to a hotel.

The SCS stereoscope acted like my old hand-held viewer with one mutation: now the camera was flying. So each scene became a relief map, each crease in the terrain tangible. Quite a step up from the topo maps published by the U.S. Geological Survey! On the table I saw the watershed as if I were floating over it in a balloon.

I asked Marckes if the ten-acre runoff was too much for the pond.

"Depends. The forest will soak up lots of water before it floods the basin. But if the land gets saturated . . ." He shrugged. "That's why it's a good idea to measure the watershed *before* you dig the pond."

Marckes handed me a sky-blue paperback brimming with graphs, diagrams, and pond-making techniques. It was called *Ponds for Water Supply and Recreation*, published by the SCS.

"You'll see formulas in here for calculating pond capacity according to the size of the watershed. I'd work it out, but I'm packing."

Marckes told me that his job at the SCS had been cut. After a year of pond work he was about to return to his family's farm in Craftsbury. Government funds had been shifted to clean up pollution, and the SCS was pulling out of pond making. Ironically, water protection had bumped off ponds.

For decades Uncle Sam was sugar daddy for country pond makers. After the dust bowl, the Department of Agriculture prescribed ponds for flooding, erosion, and drought. The Civilian Construction Corps of the New Deal built thousands of ponds across the country, and farmers received funds and technical help to carve their own reservoirs. As recently as 1975, in Vermont, the SCS contributed up to 80 percent of the funds needed for farmers to build ponds. But lately, not only farmers have wanted pond making assistance; there has been a migration of homesteaders and gardeners, and the SCS could not afford to dig ponds for them all. So, the agency tightened up funding.

The figures for Orange County tell the story. In 1977 the SCS assisted on sixty-two ponds, averaging forty hours of work on each one. In subsequent years the number dropped dramatically until, by the late 1980s, the SCS had cut their involvement to one or two ponds a year.

I was surprised. In my territory I had counted at least a dozen new ponds each summer.

"People are digging without us," Marckes said. He guessed that because the SCS had established such rigid pond-making criteria—drain-piping, for instance, was virtually compulsory—many land owners couldn't afford to build to government specifications. Instead they were designing and digging their own. It sounded like my story.

Marckes fished through a stack of papers and pulled out two fat manila envelopes.

"I've been saving these blueprints and excavation plans from my pond training. You should have them."

Then he added a batch of soil surveys, and we shook hands. "Good luck," he said. "You're on your own."

On Ice

The pond maker's Blue Book opens with a map of the United States covered with bars. The map is a dead ringer for the National Arboretum gardening guide, but instead of planting zones, the country is divided into pond zones. Each bar is a regional boundary marking the watershed required to supply one acre-foot of pond storage. An acre-foot is the equivalent of one surface acre covered with one foot of water, or a half-acre covered with two feet, etc. In each acre-foot are 325,851 gallons.

To figure acre-footage I needed to work out the surface acreage of the pond and multiply by the average depth. According to the bar slicing through my territory, the pond needed 1½ acres of watershed to feed each acre-foot. How close a match had I made?

In some circles acreage is measured by plotting terrain on graph paper, cutting out the inscribed area, and weighing the diagram on a scale. That edge of precision was beyond any kitchen balance. I considered calling the pond a circle with a diameter averaging somewhere between the longest and shortest surface crossing, and working out the formula for its area. Then I remembered that folded up in one of Marckes's envelopes was a table-sized sheet of vellum graph paper. I spread it out on the cabin floor. On one side Marckes had drawn a contour map of a pond site with shoreline and embankment elevations. The reverse side was clean. Scaled at one foot per square, there was more than an acre of paper, plenty of space to model my pond.

Winter is a fitting season for scribing a pond : the surveyor walks on water. I blazed the snow-crusted surface the same way I cut up a pie, marking off two perpendicular center lines, with two more slices to bisect the quarters into eighths. Footprints in the snow recorded the measurements for me as I paced off the distance from midpoint to shore. First I paced off the longest axis, thirty-one yards. Then I returned fifteen and one-half paces to the center to make the right-angle quartering cuts, which ran eleven and fourteen yards from the center to the opposite shores. Finding the shoreline was no trouble. Our neighborhood broom hockey squad had shoveled the pond for a couple of moonlit games, and a lip of snow curled up at the shore like the rim around a pie plate.

From the slope overlooking the pond I sighted two more lines to bisect the quarters. I tracked these additional spokes radiating from the center, ranging from eleven to eighteen paces, and turned home to transfer the dimensions to the graph. I centered the long axis on the middle line of the graph and marked it: 93 feet. I added the three other crossings: 72, 84, and 70 feet. Then I sketched in a rough shoreline connecting the eight points at the edge of the pond, emulating its egg shape in freehand connect-the-dots style. Within the circle were 36 perfect blocks of 100 squares: 3600 square feet. Around the banks were 24 incomplete blocks of differing sizes lapping the shore. I totaled the squares inside the pond: 1715 square feet. In sum, the pond surface added up to 5315 square feet, about one-eighth acre.

Knowing the surface acreage gave me half the formula for figuring acre-footage. To complete the set I had to multiply the depth of the pond at the dam by 0.4. Anyone who ever waded in a pond knows, of course, that the depth at the dam is only a few inches; pond basin walls are sloped, unlike a swimming pool's. I skimmed ahead and found a sample formula with the dam depth set at 12 feet. What seemed required was the full depth where the embankment starts to rise. With my toes in the mud near the bottom, I knew my outstretched hands reached about a foot short of the water surface: eight feet according to my steel tape. So the average depth was 3.2 feet. To finish the calculation I multiplied the average depth by the surface acreage—3.2 × ⅛—and got .40 acre-feet, or 131,340 gallons.

But the formula was flawed. The weak link was the assumption that the pond depth averages four-tenths the full depth of the bowl. In fact, no two ponds are the same, and the inside slopes vary from shallow to steep, even within the same basin. The two excavation styles, dammed and dugout, produce bowls of different shape. Dammed ponds dug from within have bowls of moderate slope, usually about 3:1. Dugouts excavated from shore by dragline have basins as steep as 2:1. So I rounded off my pond to a clean half acre-foot. The basin walls here are steeper than average, and I wanted to smooth out the math. Then I flipped back to the pond map and traced the bar running through my territory to its key. The watershed covered thirteen times the territory needed to supply a half acre-foot! It was big enough to suckle a dozen more small ponds, or a fat 1½-acre reservoir that would swallow up the cabin, the pond, and three years of clearing. Impossible! Yet there it was: 1½ acres feeds 1 acre-foot, and I had ten acres running into a half acre-foot pond.

Scanning the map I saw only three other territories with watersheds this rich: the coastal Northwest, the southern Appalachians, and Florida. Elsewhere, especially east of the Mississippi River, pond prospects looked more relaxed: four or five acres of drainage to keep up each acre-foot. Alas, was a Vermont pond maker living in a ten-acre watershed

obliged to dig a lake? I pulled up close to the woodstove and searched the Blue Book.

Private land users had built more than 2.2 million ponds in the United States by 1969 and many more will be needed in the future. . . .

The demand for water has increased tremendously in recent years. Land users have become aware of the benefits of providing water for many purposes, such as fish production, recreation, and wildlife habitats. For years farmers and ranchers have been building ponds for livestock water and irrigation. . . .

Locate the pond where the largest storage volume can be obtained with the least amount of earthfill. Do not locate your pond where the failure of the dam could cause loss of life, injury to persons or livestock, damage to residences or industrial buildings, railroads or highways. Be sure that no buried pipelines or cables cross a proposed pond site. Avoid sites under power lines. . . .

The physical characteristics that directly affect the yield of water are relief, soil infiltration, plant cover, and surface storage. Storm characteristics such as amount, intensity, and duration of rainfall also affect water yield. . . .

Average physical conditions in the area are assumed to be the normal runoff-producing characteristics for a drainage area, such as moderate slopes, normal soil infiltration, fair to good plant cover, and normal surface storage. Some adjustments may be necessary to meet local conditions. . . . Reduce the values by as much as 25 percent for drainage areas having extreme runoff producing characteristics. Increase them by as much as 50 percent or more for low runoff-producing characteristics. . . .

Low runoff! The forest here is an evergreen blotter, climax growth of balsams, hemlock, spruce, pine, and half a dozen hardwoods. The ground cover is loamy glacial till of rapid permeability. To put my mind at ease I simply had to "adjust" the watershed factor—by a factor of 1000 percent. I closed the Blue Book and got up to split a log for the fire.
   Knock on wood.

Spring

On and off through my first winter on the pond I had been hiring out as a carpenter to raise cash to patch up the hole punched in my bank account by the excavation bill. For a couple of weeks in March I lived on the outskirts of Stowe in a log house that was suffering a face-lift. When flatlanders think of Vermont, many think of Stowe. But when Vermonters think of Stowe, they think of money. I felt rich and eager to get home before I spent it all.

Sparkling corn snow lit the trail to the cabin. The moon was hanging from its zenith; it must have been around midnight. As the steep path lifted, it traversed the dam to the slope above the pond. Around the shore a bead of water framed an iridescent iceberg. The pond was shedding its winter coat. Crouching down on the bank where the ice nudged the shore, I leaned on the edge of the floating sphere. It began to glide. I pushed hard. Shimmering like a prism, the iceberg chased the moon west. I headed for the cabin and dreams of spring.

The pond broke out of its frozen pod, drawing up snowmelt until the spillway lunged out like a taproot and the water turned green. Early mornings, on my circuit to the mailbox, I watched the dam for hints of flooding and clocked the progress of the vaulting sun. Mulch hay on the steep north bank leeched into the water, igniting a bloom of emerald algae. Ahead of meadow grass and garden seed, this flare of chlorophyll was the first sign of new life on the land, as the pond joined robins, geese, and red-winged blackbirds on the early warning line for spring.

Spring runoff flowed down the spillway so serenely that I had to poke the toe of my boot into the water to be sure it was moving. Yet a few yards below the crest I saw damage. The channel had eroded as frost worked out of the ground. The flanks of the spillway slumped, and a stretch of riprap lay muscled aside where the stream had taken a shortcut.

With a shovel I flattened out the eroding banks and added another layer of stone. Again overflow climbed the shore, sluiced over the two-yard crest and spilled down the exit slope, but the channel held.

I circled the pond with a shovel over my shoulder, hunting erosion. Water sweated out around the embankment like runoff from a cold glass of beer. It seeped into a pool that fed a pair of streams gullying down the tracks in my dirt road. I etched diagonal water bars in the road to detour runoff and paid Peanut Godfrey thirty-five bucks to dump a truckload of good gravel on the soft spots. Then I focused healing rays on the pond to seal the embankment tight. Hell, gravel is an endangered species, and Peanut wanted forty a load next time—if he could find any.

Scouts

Spring poured in, and the blast effect of the groundbreaking summer smoothed out. The pond silt settled, and the water glowed green and so transparent that I could count stones eight feet down. Like yeast fallen after zymurgy in a crock of lager, sediment dusted the bottom. Tiny craters appeared where rocks had rolled and anchored down, and underwater furrows mapped the spring flow. I've seen water this clear just once—in the Caribbean bays of Carriacou Island where dories smuggling Heineken's beer seemed to levitate over the green brine.

To preserve pond clarity I raked out decaying autumn leaves from the shallows along the east shore. It wasn't a big chore; the pond was well set for self-cleaning. The valley here runs with the dominant northwest wind, and, open high on the hill, the pond is rarely becalmed. Windblown leaves sail to the east side of the pond, catch in the spillway current, and flush downstream to the south.

Under the weight of the D-6 the dam had been compressed tightly, a fine trick for holding water, but murder on topsoil and seed. The dam was soggy, with just a fuzz of vegetation to wick off water. Now it wanted strong breezes to evaporate moisture. In the spring winds that obliged, tree trunks bowed around the shore, and I retreated to the cabin for a sheltered outlook. I cranked up the piano stool for an orchestra seat at the southern windows. The sun rolled over the pond, and the wind kicked up a kaleidoscopic chop. As wind and water mixed I saw good omens for trout. Aerated water guarantees fish a strong diet of dissolved oxygen. The richer the oxygen, the better the potential for stock.

In early May I went out to test the water. In the glow of the mirrored sun I hunkered down naked on the north bank, warming up for the plunge. The pond was drawing to life. Where woodcock had nested a year ago I spotted salamanders twining underwater. My orange cat circled the pond stalking frogs, but they squeaked and splashed away. The yellow birch that I had singed with brush fire leafed out in green, and two blue jays dove in and out of its crown, carrying the makings for a nest. I ran to the edge of the bank and leaped. In the evening I bedded in a dozen fingerlings.

No single formula works for stocking fish, but there must be a million notions. At the top of the list is the precaution against stocking until a year after excavation. Evidently, stocking too soon kills fish. I've heard different explanations for this. Newly dug ponds are likely to be unbalanced on the pH scale. In acid water fish develop respiratory problems and hypersensitivity to bacterial parasites. East of the "lime line" that runs straight north from the southern tip of Texas, most ponds test acid. In Illinois, many new fish ponds become fatally acidic because of metallic ores in the ground. Strip mine pits can be reclaimed as fish ponds, but not until high acid has been buffered by incoming leaves and organic matter, or in some cases, chemicals. Other causes of acid water are inorganic fertilizers and sulphurous fungicides leaching from nearby crop land, and acid rain. Alkaline waters are more forgiving, but in the extreme they can be toxic and sterile. Flowing wells and springs may contain high amounts of sulphate, methane, and gases that elevate the alkaline content. In Florida, new ponds tend to be highly alkaline because of rich phosphorous deposits in the earth. Limestone quarry waters start off hard enough to be completely sterile.

The remedy? Like good garden soil, fertile pond water should balance acid and alkaline elements. To temper acid water, pond keepers add ground limestone or unleached hardwood ashes hauled from the wood stove. Manure and compost tend to balance both hard and soft waters. And time helps: the seasonal inflow of nutrients mellows pond water.

The correct pH depends on the type of fish being cultured. Optimum for trout is between 6 and 7—6.5 is best. Most warmwater fish like their water between 5 and 7, although they are more tolerant of extremes. Catfish, for instance, thrive between 5 and 9, with something between 7 and 8.5 best.

I wasn't worried about the pH. Like the surrounding soil that holds the pond, the pH was a bit acid, about 6. But I was concerned about oxygen levels. In Vermont, veteran pond makers know that freshly dug ponds will suffocate fish. Organic matter on the bottom, unless scraped clean, burns up oxygen in the water as it decays. Local pond makers traditionally postpone stocking until the second year, giving the water a chance to cure.

Henry Marckes had cautioned me about premature stocking. He suggested one old custom for testing pond oxygen.

"Weigh down one end of a red oak plank," he said, "and drop it to the bottom of the pond. Bring it up after a week, and if the end is discolored, it shows a lack of oxygen."

I was short a red oak plank, and lumber prices were sky-high. But the pond had eleven months' seasoning. I decided to take a chance and send out a scouting party of trout to test the water for themselves. At forty cents apiece, a couple of dozen trout promised to work as well as the best pond meter on the market, and more cheaply.

I went for the fish to the west side of Sharon Mountain, the Sunnybrook Trout Hatchery, Vermont's oldest fish farm. Sunnybrook got started more than fifty years ago when Harold Day planted a small forest of pine seedlings on the slopes around his valley stream. As the trees reached lumber girth he cut and hitched sawlogs to the mill and hauled home the lumber for his hatchery. What he couldn't make with homegrown planks and beams, he poured with forty tons of concrete. The ponds he dug by hand.

My knock at the farmhouse door awakened the eighty-year-old fish farmer from a forenoon nap on the porch. I told Day about my plan to break in the pond with a small stocking of brookies. He nodded and laced up his boots. On the way to net the fry we crossed through a field of small circular earth ponds marbled with trout. Each pond was roughly fifteen feet in diameter and three to four feet deep, with a single narrow pier running to the center of the basin. Fresh stream water splashed in by gravity-feed pipe, cooling and aerating the water, and then flowed out a return line to the stream below. Schools of trout graded to age and size filled the ponds.

"Trout like small round earth ponds the best," Day said. "They're easy to manage and easy to aerate, and you can't over-aerate a pond."

In one pond a gang of three-year old rainbows caught sight of us and gathered near the bank. Day tossed some trout food, and when it hit the water, the trout exploded. A geyser of water blew up for an instant. Then it was gone. So was the food.

"You see, you have to be careful not to overstock," he said. "Trout can bang together when they're feeding and blind themselves."

A water-level outlet poked up in the middle of each pond. Working both as a drain and a filter, the outlet drew a slow whirlpool of water to the center of the basin, catching leaves and debris on a screen. Day told me that the piers doubled as platforms for hanging woodchuck carcasses to rot and drop maggots to feed the fish. He added that he had been having trouble with poachers. A while ago he caught a heron that had been stalking the ponds, and when he shook it upside down, forty trout dropped out. Water rats and snakes also preyed on his small fry, and lately his trout had difficulty spawning. He blamed the acid rain.

We walked downstream to the raceways where the fry were swimming in long, narrow concrete stalls coursing with stream water. Here, under the cover of a post-and-beam barn frame glazed with translucent plastic, the vulnerable small trout lived safe from predators. Day picked up a fish net and walked the plank over a raceway full of four-inch brookies. He scanned the water. He was watching for fish stuck in a seam or a crack in the concrete. "Trout can't back up," he explained.

After scooping up a netful of fish, he gently tipped twenty-four fingerlings into a clear plastic bag ballasted with a few inches of fresh water. Then I followed him into a small pine-paneled shed off the north end of the raceways. He poked a rubber hose into the bag of fish, opened the valve on an oxygen tank, and blew up the sack like a balloon. Tying off the top with baling twine, he set the bag on the floor. The oxygen would keep the fish alive during the drive home, he said. For long journeys he recommended occasional stops to splash up the oxygen by hand.

"Every twenty miles or so. That's the way we used to keep them alive, shipping in milk cans."

Inside the balloon the trout jumped around and drummed water on the plastic skin. Day scooped up a coffee can full of trout chow from a feed bag.

"Once or twice a day," he said, offering the can. "No more than what they'll clean up. This will get you started."

I told Day that I hoped eventually the trout would grow on food from the pond habitat. "I don't like the taste of trout raised on factory feed."

"I like to feed them," Day replied. "But I don't eat them."

He took $9.60 for the fry, and I stuffed the balloon into the front seat of my VW bug. The trout leaped all the way home.

To ease the fish into their new home I mixed a sap bucket full of cold pond water into the sack. I was ready to pour in the trout when I remembered the spillway. I sharpened up two sticks of white birch and fenced the stream with half-inch wire mesh ripped off my cement sand sifter. Then I anchored the edge of the screen with stones, and the corral was closed. And with a splash I became a fish farmer.

From the slope over the north bay I watched the trout cautiously exploring, clumped together as tightly as they had lived in the raceways. In a constellation they made regular orbits of the pond, counter-clockwise. That seemed right. It cast them against the flow of the incoming spring. They were as easy to follow as goldfish in a bowl. Better than any aquarist, however, I had the advantage of seeing the fish in a natural habitat. Through spring the trout spread out. The school broke up into gangs of three or four fish circling the shallows, foraging the bottom, breaking the surface to snap May flies, mosquitoes, and gnats. Working in the garden, I made it a habit to pick a few worms and bugs to throw to the fish. From the cabin, ripples set off by the feeding trout looked like rain.

One morning I found a fish floating near the spillway. I

picked it up but found no sign of parasites or injury. I called Day. He told me not to worry.

"You can expect five percent mortality, that's normal."

Brook trout, in spite of the name, make good mountain pond stock. They thrive in oxygen-rich cold water, gaining weight at between 50 and 65°F. Given a seepage of spring water and a little luck, they will spawn in a pond. Not so for the rainbow female, which needs a stream current to spawn. The distinction arose during the Ice Ages, when the glaciers split them up, isolating the rainbow in warmer waters than the brook and making it more stress resistant.

Rainbows can briefly survive temperatures as high as 85°F and can put on weight over a greater range of temperatures than other trout. They are so adaptable that Norwegian fish farmers keep up with their southern competitors by shifting the rainbows from freshwater ponds in summer to sea cages in winter, where warmer temperatures keep them growing.

The brook trout is another story. His growth rate is slower than the rainbow's, and he demands colder water with rich oxygen levels. At 70°F he's stressed, and over 77°F he's dead. As if to make up for this, the brook can spawn naturally in a pond or lake, as well as in a stream. Its superiority lies in nestmaking. A female rainbow depends on the stream current to protect her eggs under silt and gravel; the brook trout uses her anal fin to scoop out and cover the nest. And at the end of the line, the brook trout is far tastier than the rainbow.

Looking over the pond I saw a distilled farm: shelter, feed, and fencing all in one. Since trout transform about 85 percent of what they eat into food, against 10 percent converted by cattle, the pond promised to grow protein more efficiently than a field. Moreover, because fish inhabit the earth three-dimensionally, they make thriftier stock than animals that tread shoulder-to-shoulder. And they are cold-blooded and float. If I had it as easy as a trout, I'd be warm year round and feel like I weighed 7½ pounds, not 150.

No wonder freshwater aquaculture is on the rise. Fish are sponges that take on the flavor of the surrounding water, and the marine fish farmer never knows where the next poison will wash up. I had carved the pond where the freshness of inflow was assured, with no sewage uphill. But I had one concern. Silt. Sonny and the dozer had stripped the sod from the stream that carried the main spring to the pond, simultaneously steepening the slope. Now the channel had eroded and a small delta of silt and sand was building at the shoreline, the first evidence of eutrophication. To buffer the incoming channel, I laid up stones like a staircase in the stream. My source was a necklace of boulders around the birch tree overlooking the pond. I planned the stones to mirror the spillway across the water, reverse image, climbing out of the pond. Both channels would reflect my effort to hold the soil: the stone spillway to keep runoff from dissolving the excavation, the stone steps to keep soil from filling it in.

I waited for a warm May morning to begin rolling boulders down the bank. In the shallow water around the spring inlet I shoveled out a footing for the first stones. Then I went prying through the rock pile, hunting flat boulders. Laying the steps was like putting together a half-ton jigsaw puzzle without a picture of the solution. All afternoon I rolled stones and dove from the rising steps. I finished, standing on the headstone six feet over the water. Down in the valley waves of clover rolled in the wind. The hills glowed grapefruit-green with leafing poplars, the first of spring. In the small plunge pool at the foot of the stones, several trout turned and fed.

Flow to the Garden

The first summer on the hill I turned over a garden and found that quenching the soil's thirst threatened to drain the spring. So I planted a few radishes and greens and sprinkled lightly to keep up a flow of summer salads. When the pond filled it looked like an invitation to beef up the crops. The catch was getting water from the pond to the garden, a steep uphill trek. Just an inch of water over the 800-square foot patch meant 450 gallons. I flirted with the notion of a wind-powered water pump at the edge of the garden until I read the price tag—some scarecrow. I could dig another pond with the money required to raise a wind-pump. It seemed that it might make more sense to dig another garden.

With two weeks until Memorial Day I had to move fast. Just one site below the pond was low enough to catch both gravity flow and sun. It was a long narrow stretch tangled up in blackberry brambles, open to the west, and sheltered by a steep bank to the east. It fielded plenty of light, which encouraged me, and strong winds, which didn't.

A neighbor was opening a logging road through his woodlot, and the pounding of the bulldozer drew me over. At the controls of the machine sat a large fellow with ear protectors over a baseball cap and a pony tail that dangled down his back. His name was Brad, and he looked pleased at the prospect of a little work just around the corner. It didn't take long to stage the garden. Brad skinned the topsoil and heaped it aside. Whittling with his four-way blade, he began to pare out the biggest boulders. I told him to use the stones to raise the west side of the garden. Tilting the bed east would deflect the wind and tip runoff back into the soil, instead of downhill. As he worked I followed, picking rocks. After a couple of hours the topsoil was back, and Brad rumbled down the road with thirty bucks in his pocket.

I bought a twenty-dollar dump-truckload of rotted cow manure from Ken Doyle's dairy farm. A scheme came to me in the midst of spreading it, so I left the south half of the garden bare. As long as I was going to irrigate greens, why not water some meat? A pig in a portable pen would fertilize and till one end, and next spring I could reverse plots and forget about calling Ken Doyle. That afternoon I caught Gerard Stevens aboard his tractor. He owed me a little for an old wood stove I had traded him, and he plowed and harrowed the garden to scratch his debt. As the sun poured its evening fire over the freshly dressed ground, I slipped off my boots and paced the earth barefoot. A frog croaked. A wave of cool moist air washed down over me from the pond.

Three thousand years ago the Chinese began connecting gardens and ponds, using bamboo raised in wetlands for piping. I plugged my garden and pond together with a ten-dollar green vinyl hose. That wasn't the only twist in this twentieth-century pond culture. Working a solo pond with trout ruled out warm-water fishes and mixed cropping. Considering the rich stews cooked up by ancient Eastern pond makers, I felt a pang of envy. Early Chinese farmers planted pond dikes with willow trees. Willow roots helped bind together a sandy embankment; branches were fashioned into fish poles, nets, baskets, paper pulp, and charcoal; the bark yielded salicin, the chemical predecessor of aspirin. Other farmers preferred to plant banana trees around ponds, claiming that water spilling off banana leaves stimulated healthy fish crops. As it happens, banana skins and stems are rich in potash, phosphoric acid, nitrogen, and bacteria, adding up to a shower of well-balanced fertilizer.

East of China, natives of the Hawaiian Islands mixed their own rich blend of pond plants and fish. Written descriptions of island ponds had to wait for the arrival of eighteenth-century Western explorers, but historians now suppose that Pacific pond culture dates back at least 2,000 years. By the time Captain Cook put Hawaii on the map in 1778, more than 200 shoal ponds—called *lokos*—circled the islands of Hawaii, Maui, Molokai, Oahu, and Kauai. Some lokos exceeded 500 acres, and fish production totaled two million pounds a year. Land with many lokos was called "fat."

Pond making was a communal project initiated by command of a regional king. Communities worked together gathering coral and rock for the dam. A dam might be raised across the mouth of a small bay or between two close points on the shore, forming a semicircular fish corral. Some dams stretched as long as half a mile and took a year to build. Like beaver dams, the barriers were constructed loosely to permit a flow-through of water. Bamboo gates in the dam were opened to the rising tide, allowing fish to swim in, and then closed. Shallow lokos worked best, producing a rich underwater crop of microbenthes, crusty growths of blue-green algae, diatoms, nematodes, and small crustaceans, which thrived within a couple of feet of the water surface. It was this underwater crop that growers cultivated to fatten their milkfish and mullet. Thus the loko worked as a fish trap and served feed simultaneously.

Hawaiians also built inland embankment ponds. These lay close to the sea, taking in salt water through ditches and fresh water from springs and streams. Fish netted from the sea grew especially fat in these brackish waters. Two huge embankment ponds in Kailau, Oahu, sustained four varieties of fish and a crop of edible algae called *limu*. A more typical inland pond, however, was a small dugout excavated in a marsh by a farmer who wanted to supplement his field crops. After stocking the pond with a few gourds of *awa* fry—milkfish—the farmer threw in a ceremonial offering of sweet potatoes. This was considered essential for a healthy crop, since it usually prevented infestations of freshwater grubs and dragonfly larvae. Ponds were planted with islands of taro, a heavy-feeding plant that natives enjoyed eating fresh or fermented into *poi*. Fish also enjoyed feeding on ripe taro stems, growing so fat and tame that they sometimes knocked over wading children.

Imagine a pond full of fish as big as pigs: it's not just Hawaiian history. Hog-sized blue catfish swam the inland waters of this country sixty years ago, along with half-ton sturgeons and two-hundred-pound paddlefish with snouts like beaver tails. But pollution killed off those giants, and small ponds now used to safeguard water yield small fish. Of course small fish have their advantages: after fattening up a hundred trout, you can take your harvest in skillet-sized servings.

I had in mind a more orthodox hog, and I built an eight-by-eight pen with balsam culls from the woods, leaving the bark intact for a back scratch. I set a galvanized watering tub in one corner and dropped in the hose with a faucet screwed to the end. Then I ran the hose up the pond embankment to the water. Standing on the dam, I looked down at the pen. With its high corner posts and rough sapling rails, it looked like an ocean fish trap waiting for the tide.

Bishop of Ponds

I named the pig The Bishop and slopped his provender with some freshly bottled stout to make it stick. The baptism happened a couple of weeks after I dropped him into the pen. He was six weeks old by then, a salmon-pink shoat reared by a neighborhood breeder. One afternoon before feeding, I watched him nose up a crater in the dirt and tip over his water tub to fill it. I sat on the dam while he wallowed in his mud pond. The timing was right. I had just finished plowing through *A New Booke of Good Husbandry*, the sixteenth-century pond keeper's handbook by the Bohemian bishop Janus Dubravius. Discussing fish diet, Dubravius distinguishes between *Supernas* and *Infernas*. From the "upper part" of the pond, Supernas is summer food: flies and gnats and worms. Infernas, winter food, "is the Slyme and Sande, such as Carpes feede on in the bottom of the Ponde . . . as the places wherein they lie are found made hollow, as swine are wont to make hollow their wallowing places." Wallowing right in front of me was the bishop's medieval vision.

"Hey, Bishop!"

The pig looked up. That was it—I fetched the stout.

After first appearing in Latin in Zurich in 1559, Dubravius's guide was reprinted three times during the next hundred years. The English translation was published in 1599. It made a fine impression on Issak Walton, who recycled portions of the material in *The Compleat Angler*. The particulars of Dubravius's life are few: Born in Bohemia, student of law in Italy, commander in battle against the Turks, Bishop of Olmutz, and buried in 1553. But his spirit comes through in the book. Dubravius concedes that ponds can be used for swimming, bathing, irrigation, cattle-watering, and fowl-raising. (Oddly, he never mentions milling.) But qualities of a different nature interest him. "Can there be a greater or more certaine example of the worthynesse of Pondes," he writes, "then that whereby not onely the owners be made rich through their yearly revenues and rentes, but the measurers and overseers be delivered from slaverie and bondage, and restored to liberty and freedom. . . ." For proof, Dubravius tells the story of William of Berenstenie. "He being required to shew his famlie, what maner of Farme he liked best: That quoth he, which hath plentie of Pondes belonging to it." Heeding William's advice, his son Janus became "the richest Ruler and Alderman of Bohemia and Moravia by the revenues of his Pondes."

What made Bohemian ponds so powerful? The German carp. With its Fu Manchu barbels and armorlike scales, this fish is the perfect draftee for a castle moat. In fact, in Japan, where decorative carp are bred for their kaleidoscopic coloring, the intimidating German carp is shunned because of its military bearing. Looks are deceiving, as Dubravius explains:

> Nature made him hue amongst other fish, without damage doing, and hurting no kinde of thing that lyeth in the water. Besides this he hath no gaping mouth armed with teeth, cut close and tender: and as often as he gapeth, his mouth is round, and shyning like a ring. He hath onely two teeth in his mouth, and those very blunt. Blunt also is his back-bone, & soft be his finnes:

and a light male covereth all his body, by reason of the continuall comunction and joyning together of the scales. Such a thing also is his forked tayle with the which he as quickly swimmeth over al the Ponde, as if he were roed in a boat: and there lyeth of his owne juice, without any cost to his Maister, bringing this commoditie, that where as he is fatted of his owne, he most delicately feedeth his maister with the pleasant and sweet foode of his body, whether it be roasted, baken, sodden, or salted.

Today in fish ponds around the world carp confirm the bishop's blessing—except in the United States, where the fish has been banished like a heretic. Game fishermen can't stand carp muddying up streams in bottom-feeding frenzies. In China, the "King of Fishes" has been the primary fish of pond culture for several thousand years. Chinese carp growers recently outproduced American catfish farmers eight-to-one per acre, feeding just grass clippings. In Israel, desert ponds full of brackish water produce more than 10,000 tons of carp annually, two thirds of the country's fish crop. Carp for the table is raised in France, Portugal, the Netherlands, West Germany, Austria, Italy, Japan, and Korea. In many of these countries, farmers raise batches of two- to three-pound carp with little or no feed.

Why is such a profitable crop banned most of the United States? Must keeping carp out of fishing streams preclude production in ponds? I asked Jim Malone, who has been raising carp for over a quarter century in Lonoke, Arkansas.

"The trouble here may be that you have an eating style already built up, and the carp doesn't fit," he said. "The problem is bone structure. The fish has thousands of bones imbedded in the flesh. The Europeans bake them and flake off the flesh, and Chinese fry up carp with rice. But it's never caught on here."

So Malone ships his fish within the legal territory for natural control of aquatic moss, weeds, and algae. His white amur, silver, and bighead are biological vacuum cleaners. In warm climates a half-pound carp will put on eleven pounds in one year. That's a lot of weeding—and meat.

Today in Eastern Europe—"Our country of Pondes," as Dubravius called it—fish farming continues, and about 70 percent of production involves carp. To achieve maximum production, fish that feed at different water levels are raised together in a polyculture. Stocking usually is about 70 percent common carp and 25 percent grass carp, with a scattering of catfish, silver carp, and pike. In Hungary, carp and ducks are cultured together; after five years the ponds are drained; for two years they are planted with alfalfa, and then for three years with rice; then they are flooded and stocked again and the cycle resumes. Little or no feed is required to raise crops in this self-fertilizing culture. Pond and field rotation is "still in the research stage," according to the Fish Culture Institute in Szarvas. Yet, if you listen to Dubravius, the formula for pond rotation was settled 400 years ago:

Pondes must be renewed & refreshed by having no moysture in them, as feeldes are by lying fallow and untylled. This intermission and drying of Pondes, is most commonly used after eight or nine years, that is to say, after foure or five lawfull fishinges: a lawfull fyshing I call every second yeeres fyshing. And this ceassing and drying of the Pondes must no longer continue then one yeere: duering all which yeere, some profit may also come therof for though the Pondes bottomes lye dry without water, yet you may sowe them with Corne, and use the crop therof. And agayne, after one Sommer be past, fyshe them, if your Carpe there put in, be of three yeeres growth. But and if your Pondes be very olde, so that they lacke force to nouryshe, and therefore are unfruitfull, then one yeeres drynesse is not sufficient, but the second and thyrde yeere you must but lightly eare up the earth, thoroughly douge it, and lastly sowe it with such feede as will easely spring up in barren ground. Of this sort is Mullet seede, and Lupines seed, which all sometimes serve for doung, as often as it is plowed together therwith. The second yeere you may sowe it with feede of more strength, and the third year with the strongest seede of all, and use the crop if you wish. And thus you may see how no year is without his profit, until such time as it is apt agayne for fyshing.

Dubravius never mentions the removal of pond sediment in his prescription for pond renewal. Considering the effectiveness of pond rotation, why should he? Basin drawdown exposes the pond to the antiseptic weathering of the sun and wind. Reeds and other unwanted aquatic weeds are choked, and unwanted fish and predaceous insects are eliminated. In the basin soil, where oxygen usually is short, exposure to air accelerates the decomposition of organic matter. When legumes are planted in the pond bottom, the nitrogen level of the soil is raised. A follow-up crop of grain further enhances pond fertilization because of plant rooting. As Dubravius saw, millet makes an especially good pond rotation crop. Today we know that millet chokes weeds, entices ducks, and provides a grain more nutritious than wheat, oats, barley, or rice.

For many of my neighboring pond keepers, as well as aquaculture scientists, rotation is a lost art. I know one local farmer who hired a dragline operator to dredge his old weed-choked pond. Then he gave away the silt. This generous fellow now has a clean pond, a fertilizer debt, and a $1000 dragline bill. The problem is not merely the influence of machinery: most people just dig one pond, and who wants to give it up for a year or longer? Even a short algae-killing drawdown can be chancy with a solo pond. My friend Steve Wetmore tried it, and halfway down he ran into a drought. To save his pond-irrigated garden, he had to let the basin refill, algae and all.

When it comes time to clean up my pond I may just drain it and dig another. Then again, if I set The Bishop and his successors in the right places, there may be a fresh pond waiting when intermission comes around.

Predators and Prey

I wake up from a nightmare of valkyries swooping down out of the sun. It's an orange summer dawn. Crazy laughter echoes over the cabin, gains pitch, and passes by. Then silence. I jump out of bed. In a moment I'm running barefoot toward the pond through the cold dew, waving my arms and cursing. A blue bird launches from a white birch below the spillway. It flaps away low and fast, cackling with a derisive rattle. I watch it skyline down the valley over the brook and disappear. But the bird will be back. The pond has been discovered by a kingfisher.

The face of the pond is untroubled. No fish scraps beneath the tree, no evidence of plunder. But I've heard that a kingfisher can dive into a pond and pluck up a fish in its beak and swallow it whole. If I lost any trout, how would I know? Counting fish is as hopeless as counting stars.

Earlier in the spring, up the road at Miller Pond, I witnessed my first kingfisher attack. A state hatchery truck rumbling through the valley caught my eye, and I followed. When I pulled in at the boat landing, the truck was backed down to the water's edge. At the back of the truck a biologist was netting trout fingerlings out of a vat and ladling them into the pond. For someone accustomed to watching seining operations where fishermen haul up fish by the netful and dump them into the truck, it was a strange sight. As the biologist scooped out the last of the trout and the water behind the truck simmered with confused fingerlings, I saw a bright blue flash. A bird boomeranged off the water and streaked toward the trees across the pond. Then I heard a jubilant shriek, and more laughter from the treetops.

The biologist shrugged.

"I just put in four thousand fingerlings," he said. "There should be plenty for everyone."

Still, it wasn't his nickel. I was feeling protective about my trout crop and asked how the state hatcheries defend against kingfishers.

"Trout are pretty vulnerable at first," he admitted. "They're growing so fast that they don't have much intelligence. When a kingfisher hits, they ball up in a knot and won't feed. Later on they get to be quite smart. In Salisbury we used to trap kingfishers until they got wise to the traps. My boss is a bird lover so he wouldn't let me shoot at them. But when I showed him that the losses for the summer were five thousand fry, he changed his mind."

Shooting kingfishers is not standard pond keeping procedure. The 1918 Migratory Bird Treaty Act makes it a federal crime to kill kingfishers, herons, and gulls. Nonetheless, exceptions are made.

"At some of our hatcheries where birds are very troublesome, we have permits," he said. "If you have a commercial operation that is threatened, perhaps the U.S. Fish and Wildlife Service will issue a permit. But we suggest you use whatever scare tactic will work."

I had no urge to murder kingfishers. Besides, in a couple of months I hoped to have my trout fry nursed up to five or six inches, big enough to defend themselves and too big to slide down a kingfisher's gullet. Meanwhile, with the state doing such a good job of feeding the birds, I figured that I had a fighting chance to keep kingfishers off the pond.

There are several traditional strategies for fending off

flying predators. Some people stock bigger trout, five- to seven-inch fry. But they cost more and diminish the potential reward of the harvest. That's no solution for anyone planning to hatch fry of his own. Tree perches, especially the dead branches that kingfishers favor, can be culled from around the pond. However, clear-cutting the shelter belt around a pond seems impractical; trees often provide pond bank reinforcement, as well as shade and a place to hang a hammock. Automatic noisemakers powered by gas cartridges can be set to explode or screech at different intervals; but the birds, if not the pond keepers, are said to become used to the racket. Hatchery professionals cover raceways with netting or wire mesh, or enclose them in a building. And ponds are sometimes overrun with parallel strings crossing overhead on poles twenty to sixty inches apart, like horizontal barrage balloon wires.

I find an antidote that appeared in *Small Farmer's Journal* more appealing. Writing about pond defense, John W. Ball mentions an Oregon neighbor with a rifle-powered cure-all. His friend's pond is in full view of his house, about 400 yards away. With binoculars he can keep an eye out for predators. On the far side of the pond stands an oil barrel with a target painted on the side. One end of the drum is cut out. The barrel hangs upside down on a six-foot tree stump, a huge bell riddled with bullet holes. A couple of signs hang nearby: "Private Rifle Range—Unauthorized Persons Trespass At Their Own Risk." Ball writes, "He explained that these signs seemed to remain in place, although trespass signs along the county road disappeared at intervals. But perhaps the letters weren't significant, for the resonance sent herons, mergansers, and kingfishers with wings flapping to more peaceful areas; and on one occasion, some unidentified critters, with flapping beards, abandoned their seine and fled in a van that had been parked where the roadside signs wouldn't stay. They stay better now."

Fish is not the only crop that needs protection from predators. Young waterfowl are vulnerable to attack by hawks, and pond keepers fend them off with the same devices that repel kingfishers. Alarms and strings won't keep out a dog, however, so fencing is used. Where it is undesirable to fence a pond all around, waterfowl can be confined to a shoreland corral that overlaps a limited stretch of water.

Another dog-defense system was disclosed to me by Sherm Stebbins, a pond maker from Randolph, Vermont. A bird lover in Weston, Connecticut, had hired Sherm to dig a network of lagoons to make a waterfowl refuge. When the landowner began to worry that the birds would be devoured by neighborhood dogs, Sherm gave it some thought and finished the ponds by surrounding them with a ten-foot moat. The dogs stayed out.

Sherm told me that he had been attracted to ponds in a predatory way himself.

"I got to know the people at the bank because they were lending me money for excavating equipment. One day they called me up and asked me to build a pond on some land they'd repossessed. They couldn't sell the place. Well, the pond helped make the sale, and they made three hundred percent profit on the pond alone. After that, whenever they had trouble selling land, they hired me to dig a pond."

That was 900 ponds ago, and predators have a way of becoming prey. The last time I talked to Sherm he announced plans to retire from the pond making business. He had just returned from Beltsville, Maryland, where he had failed to convince Soil Conservation Service policy makers to regionalize construction standards for pond makers, instead of slapping uniform soil discharge rates across the whole country.

"Today the bureaucratic regulations make it impossible to keep up," he complained. Cracking a smile, he added, "I never got rich digging ponds. But I dug a lot of ponds. That's my legacy."

Blending In

The crest of summer: bean poles and potato plants showered with blossoms and, thanks to an early morning hosing during a June frost, melons and squash flower, too. Celery grows on an island collared by an irrigation trench. Evenings, I open the faucet on the hose and drop it in the trench; mornings I close it. The celery shoots up. A spray of water knocks Colorado beetles right off the potatoes. A couple of days ago I mailed off an order for a Y coupling and fifty feet of drip hose to run through the melon patch. This is polyculture by hose.

Along the outer rim of the dam I'm picking peas off a fence. At the embankment edge runoff drains away from the basin, so no fertilizer leeches into the pond. The embankment wicks up enough moisture from the pond to keep the peas well irrigated most of the time, but during a parch I water by hand. Peas make a good dam crop. They fix nitrogen in the soil and they come up early. By the time the water gets up to skinny-dipping temperature, the pond is curtained in green. Can you top a fence that hoists itself and makes delicious soup?

The dam is surprising. I withheld nutrients from the crusty topsoil to preserve water clarity, and it started out an eyesore. Soggy in wet weather, dusty hardpan in dry. I kept my focus on the water. Gradually the hay mulch has broken down, and the rye and clover are coming in strong, along with dandelions and black-eyed susans. On the outside of the bank I planted strawberries, a good perennial crop for an incline of acid soil. The dam is ripening into a vast raised bed of wildflowers, berries, and sugar snap peas.

On the other side of town Woody Ransom bulldozes new hayfields for his dairy farm. "My dream is to drive as far and as straight as I can without turning," he tells me. In the process of terracing the fields, Woody dug a mile of drainage canals and several small ponds. His whimsical contribution to aquaculture was a pair of Muscovy ducks launched a while back. Now there's a flock overrunning the farm, to the delight of his children and his cats.

So which comes first, the raised terrace or the pond? The Chinese pond maker might answer: Neither, they're synonymous. Ancient Chinese town builders commenced work with the excavation of a deep moat around the site; then earth dug from the moat was used to build a defensive wall. When Marco Polo returned to Venice from his Asian explorations, among the wonders of China he reported seeing was a hill "made by art" from the earth dug out of a lake excavation. The hill sat about a bowshot away from the palace of the Khan of the Mogol Dynasty. Polo wrote, "It is a good hundred paces in height and a mile in compass." To picture the lake, invert the hill and fill with water.

Out on the dam, I'm propping up the sagging pea fence against the weight of six-foot vines. I haven't seen a fish in days. I begin to pace the dam, searching the water. Nothing. I step to the top of the waterfall for a sight line to cut the sun's glare. The view to the bottom opens up. The trout have vanished. Did the kingfisher finish his mission while I was out? I put on my mask and jump. Swimming down to the basin floor I extend my arms. An inch from my fingers a trout darts away. Then another. Sunlight filtering through the water illuminates their spines, dappled in shades of sand

and clay. The fish look precisely like the bottom of the pond. They are dressed in camouflage.

A fish tale explains it: Once upon a time a young angler was working the Test, an English trout stream. A dark trout stood out in the clear water. The fisherman began casting. No luck. Again and again he tried, but the fish would not budge. Along came an old man who watched this lackluster contest briefly, then stepped up to the young angler and tapped him on the shoulder. "You'll never have a chance with him," he said. "He's blind."

Brian Curtis recalls that morning on the Test in his book, *The Life Story of the Fish*. He learned that day that most trout change color to protect themselves, like chameleons. Naturally, to produce camouflage they need to see. The blind trout stood out like a black olive in a dry martini. The moral? In the ken of the fly fisherman, it pays to be a blind trout. Here, in the realm of the kingfisher, I was glad to see the trout blending in.

Perhaps it was fisherman's luck that turned my cabin into a watchtower over the water. Or magic. I had staked the foundation with no thought of a pond. Now I wouldn't have it any other way. Living over water is the greatest delight of inhabiting mountain terrain—a pleasure I share with ancient kings who raised "spirit towers" over their ponds. The notion that divine spirits inhabited ponds was strong through Asia and continues today in Buddhist strongholds. In China, Tibet, and Japan, towers and temples rose over natural and man-made spirit ponds. These ponds were considered to be the dwellings of invisible water dragons, oracles, and protective goddesses, not to mention fantastic schools of very real iridescent goldfish and carp bred in dazzling colors and shapes. A bit of jade tossed into one of these ponds was hoped to bring a Chinese woman good luck in love, which might come in handy if she happened to catch the eye of Emperor Te Tsung; he kept his harem marooned in the Pondweed Palace on an island in a pond north of Changan.

In Tibet, ponds and lakes were consulted for signs of future events and reincarnations. The Dali Lama was chosen in consultation with an oracle lake called Lhamo Latso, home of his goddess protectress Pandam Lhambo. And when the Dali Lama took his place as Buddhist leader, he lived in the Potola Palace in Tibet's capital, Lhasa, overlooking Serpent Lake. According to the elder brother of the currently exiled Dali Lama, it is:

> a perfect little lake barely three hundred yards long. This is one of the lovliest parts of the city . . . in the middle is Lo Khang, or House of the Serpent. Plants and flowering shrubs seem to grow more richly here than anywhere else, and on a still day the Serpent Lake reflects the image of the Potola towering above it. This is the place the people of Lhasa love to visit during the summer, both to worship in the little island temple and simply enjoy themselves.

Pond spirits were also revered by Chinese poets, who loved their water almost as much as their wine. Many were the unknown poets of the *Shih Ching*, the oldest anthology of Chinese songs and a main text of Confucian education. Here is some of the ballad of "King Wen's Spirit Tower":

> *He measured out his spirit tower*
> *Measured it and planned it;*
> *All the people rushed to work*
> *And they built it in a day . . .*
> *Doe and stag so sleek*
> *And the white birds glisten.*

The king stands by his spirit pond
Where fishes leap around.

Taoist recluse Ch'ang Chien wrote of the solace a pond held for common folk in "Visit To The Broken Hill Temple":

At the break of day I come to an old temple
As the first rays of the sun glow on the treetops.
A path in the bamboo grove leads to a quiet retreat—
A meditation hall hidden behind flowering boughs.
Here, mountain scenery delights the birds,
And the reflections in the pond empty a man's mind.

Most magical of water bards, perhaps, was Han Yu:

In dawn's light I close my books and sit
watching the high ridges of the Southern Mountains
below which, the clear pool's water
where dragons, chilled cold can be caught. . .

Often, old poets turned to water at the end. Lying ill in a boat on Lake Tung Ting, Tu Fu wrote his last poem:

Floating, floating, what am I like
between earth and sky, a gull alone.

Indeed, many Chinese were buried with a bowl of water and a pair of fish to guarantee eternity in a spirit tower overlooking their own pond.

And what do my neighbors make of pond spirits? One summer day I took a look, flying over the Green Mountains with a friend who needed to pad his log book. I marked our chart with ponds so that in the twilight we could find our way home down a path of silver-blue reservoirs. Sheets of water waved across the horizon, mountains of ponds. I remember two especially. The first was raw, just beginning to fill. In its shallows flashed an image of white birch trees. At the other end a dragline excavator cast and reeled his steel clamshell. We took a slow turn over the pond, admiring the work of an earth sculptor with a purpose. Gravestones in a country cemetery marked the watershed surrounding the other pond. Monuments stood reflected in a liquid mirror, and the grassy banks grew thick and green: mountain spirits blending into their own reflections.

Part II
Pond Sculpture

Pondscapes

Ponds for Waterfowl and Wildlife

Siting

Excavation

Spillways

The Digger: A Stream Pond That Carves Itself

Here pond maker Ray Uline begins to carve out a quarter-acre reservoir in Lyme, New Hampshire, with his pet seven-ton Cat. "She's a good ol' gal," says Ray. "Hardly ever gets stuck, long as you mind what you're doing." Working in the spring-fed sidehill hollow, he uses the solo bulldozer to chisel the pond, from site clearing through final landscaping. In classic hill country style he takes up the earth excavated from the basin to make the embankment for this "dug-and-dammed" impoundment. As Ray shapes the dam on the downhill side of the site, he keeps a drainage ditch open in the center. Thus watershed runoff and springflow stream out of the excavation, keeping the muddy basin firm enough to support the bulldozer. No precious time is lost hauling the machine out of the muck.

Scraping bottom in the pond basin Ray searches for flaws in the earth seal—clusters of pervious stone or gravel that would be the source of potential leaks. He carves out these patches and substitutes watertight soil. A good seal is the best defense against seepage. Pond makers who claim they can waterproof impossible sites with chemical additives and underwater dynamite blasts should run out of town. Like a potter's bowl, the earth pond is molded with a blend of materials. In addition to drawing a sufficient supply of water, this site consists of good watertight soil: about 10 to 20 percent clay and an even mix of silt, sand, and gravel. Preliminary test holes in the pond basin are crucial in evaluating the worthiness of a site.

Holding water after a storm, the pond shows an early sign of success. Later, after it has filled and the silty water has cleared, brook trout will be stocked. They will find shade and shelter under the twin boulders that Ray saddled on the shoreline. With some luck, the trout will spawn their eggs in the gravel bed that he carefully spread over the incoming spring channel. While Ray finishes up the dam, a young neighbor tests the waters.

Like a sculptor driving a roaring six-foot chisel, Ray rides above his giant blade, filling in the draining ditch and shaping the slope of the earth embankment. "My ponds have lots of character," he says. "I give them a special curve." To prevent the dam from eroding, Ray abides by a cardinal rule of pond making: Bank the dam no steeper than 3:1.

Throughout the foundation of the dam, topsoil, stumps, and roots have been cleared to help the embankment adhere to the ground. As the rim of the pond is raised, the weight of the bulldozer packs the earth, making the enclosure watertight. Here at the north end of the dam, Ray uses his blade like a trowel to seal the butt joint that splices the embankment to the hillside. This seam usually makes the best site for the earth spillway, since the slope provides a natural stronghold against erosion. An overland spillway is preferable to underground plumbing, which can double the cost of a pond this size and leak, to boot.

Cloud in the ground, the newborn pond will work wonders for its owners, who plan to build a house overlooking the water. Cool swimming holes inspire hot summer carpenters and store water for mortar mixing, gardening, and chilling homebrew. For settlers, pond sculpture often precedes ground breaking for a home. A note for gamblers: According to a rough rule of thumb, the value of a finished pond is triple its construction cost.

Pondscapes

I was surprised recently to hear from a landscape gardener that her most frustrating clients were pond owners. "They have all that potential and what do they do? Nothing."

She complained that half her customers owned ponds but they had been frightened by warnings against planting trees in the embankment or using fertilizer on plants. Consequently they put down a little grass and that was it. The result, as she put it, is "that awful military look."

She has a point. Large country ponds must be landscaped differently than water garden pools designed exclusively for planting. Because reservoir builders advise against planting trees in pond dams to prevent roots from disturbing the watertight seal, embankments often look like burial mounds. Similar precautions against trees and shrubs that might load the pond with leaves, or plant fertilizer that could trigger algae, result in even more spartan layouts. What can the pond owner or landscape designer do to enhance the beauty of these backyard waterfronts without detracting from water quality or structural integrity?

Pond aesthetics begins with structural shape. "There ought to be a law against round ponds," a friend of mine says, and I've heard from plenty of pond builders and owners who agree. Nature doesn't make perfectly round ponds, the argument goes, so why should we? One contractor I know took pride in giving his ponds a "special curve." Rather than base his designs on contour surveys or drawings, he bulldozed them out by instinct, and his curves were used to add a bay or a spit of land to provide a vantage point over the water. Another local pond builder liked to dig his reservoirs in the shape of Vermont. Alas, not all contractors are that artistic. One of my neighbors was having a pond built on his place several years ago, and couldn't get through to the contractor that he wanted the shore to meander a bit as it circled the pond. "He just didn't seem to see the curve when I explained it to him, so I got up on the bulldozer and we did it together," he recalled.

Of course the shape of a pond will be dictated by the terrain, and if the lay of the land suggests a circle, why fight it? One new pond in my neighborhood looks as if it were laid out with a compass, a perfect ring. But it reads nicely, balanced by the irregularities of the surrounding hills and forest. Also, a round pond is often the most efficient shape if you're looking for size, depth, and steep sides to thwart aquatic vegetation. Keep in mind, irregular shapes that create isolated pockets of semistagnant water will encourage algae and weeds.

A square or rectangular pond has a mechanical look that's out of place in most backyards, although fine for aquaculture or cattle. A pond that is in view of a house can benefit from creative shaping. For instance, a narrow pond viewed along its axis will appear larger than if viewed across. Also, the fewer the trees around the pond, the larger the pond appears. Usually the more sky reflected in the water, the larger the pond appears.

These are all factors to consider when siting a house in relation to an existing pond. Ideally, the home-pond alignment should be on a north-south line with the pond to the south. That way both sun and water are in focus together. This alignment is in tune with solar-oriented housing principles, as well as the ancient traditions of *feng shui* and geomancy, which stress proper placement to augment spiritual energy.

Pond freeboard is an important factor in appearance. Freeboard is the amount of embankment or rim above water level. Sometimes ponds are built with exaggerated freeboards of two or three feet to ensure against flood waters breaching the dam. Unfortunately, this produces a crater-like appearance, suggesting that the pond has a leak. It also creates steep shore slopes that make it difficult for you to walk along the water's edge. One of the great pleasures of strolling by a pond is being able to amble along the shoreline observing the wildlife and vegetation in the edge area. I would rather see a gradual slope on the shoreland that encloses the pond. One pond designer I know calls this the

"brimful effect." If the pond outlet and emergency spillway are properly designed, high water during a storm shouldn't jeopardize the pond. Keep in mind that the slope of the basin underwater shouldn't be quite so gradual; a slope of 2:1 or 3:1 will discourage weeds and algae.

Excavated ponds that don't require much embankment construction present a unique landscaping problem: what to do with the excavated earth? Often pond dredgings can be used to level off nearby terrain or otherwise improve the landscape. Sometimes the earth must be trucked off-site. Whatever you do with it, don't have the material pushed up around the perimeter of the pond. Your mountainous pond shore will attract more attention than the pond itself.

Stones along the pond shore are sometimes used to enhance the natural appearance of a man-made pond. Land-

scape architects often bunch stones together to dramatize the pond shore, and in fact artificial lightweight "stones" are available from several landscaping firms. In my experience large shoreline stones—real stones—make fine diving rocks when sited at the edge of deep water. The right stone can make a fine place to sit as well as provide shade for fish. A cluster of stones lying deep on the pond bed also creates a cool water shelter for fish. Stones also can be used to build steps that lead down into the water for swimmers.

To improve access and dress up a pond, lay down a stretch of sand and create a beach. In new ponds, a beach is carved out a couple of feet deeper than the shoreline and sand is filled in. This creates a pad shallow, easy-on-the-feet of sand that also mulches out aquatic weeds and algae, otherwise a potential problem in such a shallow area. Sand can also be applied along the shore of an existing pond. Beaches are often sited on the north end of ponds so that swimmers and sunbathers are oriented sunward. Be careful not to lay down a beach in a soggy area where springs flow into the pond, or on a shore with steep banks.

Islands are often used to add to the beauty of a waterscape, particularly in water gardens and Japanese garden pools. Islands have the added benefit of providing refuge for waterfowl. In my experience, not many country ponds benefit from islands. When you go to the trouble and expense of building a reservoir, it doesn't make much sense to subtract a substantial portion of the water volume. Particularly worrisome is an island that adds to the shallow shoreline area where weeds and algae thrive. However, islands can enhance wildlife ponds.

If the terrain is suitable, waterfalls can be constructed to cascade in and out of a pond, unless inflow and outlet piping preclude it. Often the inflow is channeled in a pipe or canal to a release point where the water then falls over a series of stones or straight into the water. Water splashing into the pond has the added effect of raising the dissolved oxygen level, benefiting fish and water quality. When outlet piping is not required, a natural waterfall may be designed as the primary spillway. I know one pond owner who had an overflow pipe removed simply because she preferred to see the water leaving the pond. She then had a stone-lined channel constructed over the embankment, with a handsome iron footbridge across it. In situations where vehicles must cross the spillway, piping may be necessary.

Footbridges across inflows and outflows, or to an island, are often designed to add an aesthetic as well as practical dimension to ponds. The arched footbridges seen at Japanese garden pools were designed to appear graceful and lift the visitor higher over the water, where the view was enhanced and reflections enlarged. The arch strengthened the bridge. It's possible today to buy prebuilt arched bridges through garden supply catalogs and landscape design suppliers. Sometimes a large flat stone can be used to bridge a pond stream. Stone, steel, and iron have an advantage over wood because they won't rot. Wooden bridges should be installed so that they are supported on stone or concrete. Be careful about using preservatives on wooden bridges; toxic runoff may contaminate the pond.

Other structures that can enhance pond appearance include piers and docks. Few outdoor scenes rival a pond with a wooden plank pier and a rowboat or canoe tethered alongside. A floating dock in the middle of the water is another attractive addition to the pondscape, creating an island that's enjoyable for swimmers or waterfowl, yet won't serve as a medium for weeds and algae. It's also removable, and thus needn't get in the way of winter skating. Moreover, the shade a floating dock provides in summer can be beneficial to fish. Piers can even be built on wheels so they can be relocated or removed. They last longer that way, too. People who don't want to bother building a dock or pier often dress up a pond with a canoe or rowboat. I've seen plenty of tiny ponds you could hardly squeeze a dingy into decorated with a boat artfully beached on shore.

Ponds and garden pools require a continual flow of fresh water to maintain aquatic health. Over the past decade or two, as ponds have been used increasingly to produce fish crops, the requirements for water quality control also have increased.

High-powered aerators have been designed to oxygenate

When landscaping is an important design consideration, a visible spillway with bridge is often preferable to an underground pipe.

and circulate the water. Not only fish farmers are using these aerators. Pond builders and landscape architects have begun to use splash aerators for their decorative fountain effect. It's not unusual to see golf course ponds and other public waters stirred by these mechanical geysers.

Numerous manufacturers are designing aerators specifically for the landscaping market, with a variety of fountain effects and multi-colored lights. Aerators have a pleasant cooling and humidifying effect on the pond area and add an enjoyable splashing sound. The real beauty of these illuminated aerators is that at the same time they're attractive to look at, they're improving fish habitat and reducing algae without the use of toxic chemicals.

The combination of water and soil makes a pond environment ideal for trees, shrubs, and other plants. Ponds have been the focus of gardening artistry for centuries, most notably the ancient garden and fish pools of Japan and the reflecting ponds of Great Britain. Today in this country it's unusual to find a landscape project that doesn't include a pond-and-plant combination. And yet, ironically, there isn't a more challenging project for the country pond owner than using plants to enhance the pondscape. At the same time that a plant or shrub can beautify a pond, the nutrients it requires and its potential to spread may threaten water quality. This may be of little concern to someone creating a pool for gardening alone. Water garden pools are usually rather small, and filters, water circulation systems, and chemicals are often used to control algae and weeds. But a pond that is to be used for swimming, and perhaps raising fish, is another story.

I don't know many people who want to swim in a pond that's been treated with chemicals, even short-term herbicides that are reputed to break down into harmless components after a few days. Fish and waterfowl will almost certainly be poisoned by these chemicals, and the plant life that is killed usually settles on the pond bed where it feeds a new generation of weeds and algae.

Thus it becomes important in the landscaping of a country pond to choose plants carefully, selecting the ones that least threaten water quality. If you're not familiar with a particular variety, look for it at a local grower, particularly one that caters to water gardeners.

Iris is one of the most popular flowering pond plants, usually doing well along shore without rapidly spreading. Lupines like wet soil and, although they will spread, can easily be controlled. On the other hand, cattails can be a real nuisance if not carefully managed. The water lily is an attractive, sweet-scented pond plant that may cover shallow areas of the pond if not controlled. Lilies are often set out in shallow water in containers to prevent spreading. Containers make it possible to stock tropical varieties such as night-blooming water lilies, which can be removed for overwintering inside. Containers also make it possible to provide pockets of rich soil.

When planting seeds around a pond, work up the soil much the same way you'd prepare a vegetable garden. Simply scattering seeds on the ground won't yield much. Keep in mind that newly planted tubers, bulbs, and roots may tend to float up out of the soil or mud, or be displaced by waves. Root stock also makes attractive food for wildlife. To help ensure success you can weigh down the root or tuber by fastening on a small object such as a metal washer attached with a rubber band.

As an alternative, roots and tubers can be planted in burlap bags weighed down with gravel and soil. Several roots can be bagged together and tossed in the water where they will sink and sprout. Be sure not to plant too thinly. Pond vegetation does better in concentrated masses. In some areas where wildlife is a problem, young plants may need protection within a wire mesh or nylon netting enclosure, much as blueberries are protected from birds.

It's important to set out roots and tubers in rich soil that is suited to each species. The lotus, for instance, likes rich soil without humus or peat. The lotus is a fragrant pond favorite with both hardy and tropical varieties. Tropical varieties of the lotus and waterlily offer a greater spectrum of color than the hardier sort. The marsh marigold is a spring-blooming, yellow-flowered plant that thrives in a wet environment; while capable of spreading, it is rather easy to control. Day lilies are attractive pond-bank flowers and won't overrun the shoreland. Other plants that do well in a pond environment include mint, hosta, astilbe, rodgersia, and ferns. Because the hosta shades nearby plants, it can be an effective natural weed suppressant. Also, take note that mint can be invasive.

Ornamental grasses and wildflower mixes can add a special dimension to the pond because of their swaying motion in a wind. Marginal shrubs also should be considered, especially fruiting plants such as cranberry and blueberry. Keep in mind that shrubs and berries can provide a hedge for privacy. A few apple trees may add to the nutrient load when their leaves shed, but many people consider it a worthwhile tradeoff for the beauty of the spring blossoms reflected in the water and floating on the pond.

Other plants that will attract wildlife as well as beautify the landscape are described in the next chapter.

Because many pond owners try to avoid water problems created by fertilizers, pond plants often do poorly. Here are a few techniques to improve results. Make sure to match plants with your climate zone. Try to choose naturally rich soil areas. Planting in shady areas, sandy seeps, or gravel isn't likely to lead to success. Ponds are often sited in clayey areas. Clay is great for holding water, but it won't help plant growth much. A friend of mine planted a hedge of lilacs on his pond dam but they refused to grow in the clay soil.

Pond owners who find that grass can't get a foothold in embankment soils compacted by construction machinery often lay down sod. This is especially helpful for new ponds with erosion problems. Plants such as water lilies and lotus can be potted in containers of rich soil and then set in the pond to improve growth and control dispersal. Larger containers and trenches filled with rich soil can also be used to provide localized growing areas. Plants that require fertilizer can be set in a slight depression on shore to prevent nutrients from leaching into the water.

A veteran pond designer and former Soil Conservation Service agent I know has a list of "don'ts" for pond owners interested in landscaping. Don't plant anything tall, deep-rooted, or "dirty." Dirty, he explained, means trees like willows and pines that shed foliage into the pond and darken the water. When I asked what plantings are acceptable, he mentioned bird's-foot trefoil and short grasses like creeping red fescue, June grass, and Canadian blue. Don't forget bulbs, he added. Unfortunately that's a rather limited palette for the new breed of pond gardener, like my landscape designer friend.

Ideally, there's a happy medium between keeping the water clean and also enjoying the potential of pond plantings. In the end there's just one way to find out. Dig in.

Ponds for Waterfowl and Wildlife

From the air the prairie pothole region of northern Minnesota appears long on prairie and short on potholes. Over the past fifty years the farmers of Becker County have ditched and drained this natural slough to accommodate their wheat and corn crops. A region that once helped sustain as much as half the continent's waterfowl has become a dried-out detour sign.

Yet, magically, a new aerial film shows the brown fields suddenly transformed into a patchwork of blue ponds and marshes. In "The Hamden Slough," waves of sparkling water sweep across the screen as a restored waterfowl refuge floods the land. This is electronic sorcery, a blend of airborne camera work and computer simulation.

It's part of an effort by the U.S. Fish and Wildlife Service to enlist public support for a revival of the pothole region. The imaginary bird's-eye view dramatically conveys the healing power of water, and, if the scheme pans out, the new 8,500-acre Hamden Slough Refuge will provide cover and feed for mallard, canvasback, and redhead ducks, blue-winged teal, geese, and other threatened waterfowl. Along with the U.S. Fish and Wildlife Service, landowners across the country are excavating and restoring ponds and woodlands in similar efforts to counter threats of wildlife extinction.

Many ponds are designed and managed exclusively to attract waterfowl. Pat Kester, of Kester's Wild Game Food Nurseries in Omro, Wisconsin, says an increasing percentage of her customers are individuals managing their own ponds. The objective may be to create a protective refuge for waterfowl or lure them for hunting—perhaps both—although Kester notes that over the last ten years "there's been a breakaway from hunting." She adds that her newest clients are managers of natural filtration systems for wastewater. Many wild-game food plants have the capacity to help purify polluted water by absorbing contaminants and releasing oxygen, which supports organisms that feed on pollutants like phosphorus and nitrogen compounds.

There are numerous structural elements and plant varieties that can be incorporated into pond designs to help attract birds and other critters. Depth is an important factor. According to the Kester Nursery catalog, areas with water between six inches and three feet deep are needed to grow the aquatic plants that wild birds require. These shallow areas encourage algae and weeds, which keep swimmers away. If you're serious about creating a wildlife pond, don't expect it to be a swimming pool. Waterfowl and fish make a better combination.

Rich soil will encourage growth in the plants you set out. However, be sure the pond includes at least one area of gravel accessible to the birds. Waterfowl require grit for their digestion. Check that the water, pond bed soil, and shoreland offer a healthy pH level for growth. Kester finds that unless there is runoff from a farm or chemicals are used, freshwater ponds don't usually need treatment. She suggests that a pH level of about seven suits most plantings. Agricultural limestone is recommended to balance low pH waters polluted by acid precipitation. Be careful also about fluctuating water levels that might dry out or flood the

Cattails and other aquatic vegetation around a pond offer wildlife the food and cover they need to thrive.

plants you've established. Once the plants have matured it's likely they can withstand spring flooding.

Sago pondweed is one of the best all-around aquatic plants, producing both seeds and tubers that nourish ducks, geese, and fish. This submerged plant also provides cover for fish and helps oxygenate the water. Sago pondweed is very hardy and grows in most kinds of pondbed soils.

Wild celery is another good submerged waterfowl plant. Its seeds and tubers are enjoyed by birds, and the plant offers cover and food for fish. Wild celery grows in water from one to three and a half feet deep.

Coontail, elodea, and muskgrass are important submerged plants for waterfowl feed. In addition to providing nourishment, they oxygenate the water and provide cover for young fish. Because muskgrass may impart an off flavor to fish, it is not recommended for game-fish ponds.

The Wapato duck potato, also known as arrowhead, produces food enjoyed by waterfowl and also has attractive leaves and flowers. Its tubers were a valuable food for American Indians. Duck potato is very hardy and likes rich soil.

Wild Japanese millet is an excellent seed provider for waterfowl. Millet grows best in damp areas or along the banks of rivers or lakes. The soil should be worked before planting. Several other varieties of millet offer seeds attractive to songbirds and mammals as well as ducks.

Wild rice is one of nature's top waterfowl foods. Wild rice can be established in pond water six to eighteen inches deep as long as there is a healthy exchange of fresh water. Landlocked ponds are not suited to wild rice cultivation. In addition to providing grain, the wild rice plant offers shelter.

Plants that dress up the pond as well as offer wildlife cover and food include the lotus, waterlily, and iris. The pickerel plant and burr reed are valuable waterfowl feed and cover plants. Cattails provide excellent cover in addition to ornamentation. Other pond plants that waterfowl find attractive include smartweed and bulrush.

Waterfowl will also be attracted to plants that grow on the shoreland beyond the pond. False bittersweet is an ornamental climbing vine with purple flowers that will grow in a variety of soils, producing red berries that cling to the vine during winter. Waterfowl as well as pheasants and partridge enjoy the fruit. The American high-bush cranberry is a tall shrub that produces attractive white flowers in spring and red berries in fall. The berries last through the winter, offering food during the lean months. The berries also can be harvested for human consumption. Perennial ground covers that produce feed attractive to waterfowl include bird's-foot trefoil, flat pea, and reed canary grass.

Predatory animals, including dogs, raccoons, foxes, coyotes, and fishers, will find your nicely fattened waterfowl and their eggs tempting fare. There are a couple of ways to control predation. Waterfowl ponds usually include at least one island as refuge, often more than one to accommodate the needs of territorial nesting birds. The islands themselves offer some food and cover. Nesting boxes create a safe habitat for breeding ducks, particularly the wood duck and merganser. These shelters are often installed on tree trunks by the water's edge or on poles in the water. A metal collar below the nesting box will keep out predators, especially raccoons. Electric fences also can be installed to fend off animals.

Plenty of pond owners are happy to allow all animals free access to the water. Deer will be attracted by perennial grasses such as red and white clover, bird's-foot trefoil, and alfalfa. Muskrats like cattails, waterlily, lotus, iris, and millet. Because muskrats can damage a pond embankment digging their homes, it's not wise to encourage these crea-

tures in dammed ponds or ponds where such holes might lead to significant leakage.

Beavers may cause problems by plugging outlets to raise the water levels and thus damage the structure or territory downstream. A bacteria transmitted by beavers can infect swimmers and lead to serious illness.

When beavers become a problem, pond owners often resort to lethal means to remove them. It's not unusual to hear stories of shooting, beaver lodges blown up with explosives, water drained from ponds in winter to eliminate habitat, and even oil poured in the water. Fortunately, a more humane recourse is usually available. State fish and game wardens often will help trap and relocate the animals.

Pond owners who wish to accommodate beavers should install anti-trash guards on outlets to prevent damming. One of the most successful techniques involves building special flumes to carry overflow out of the pond, over the beaver dam. The flumes are boxed in on three sides, with wire mesh bottoms. Because beavers don't like to work on their backs upside down, they have a hard time plugging these outlets.

One of the most appealing parts of pond ownership is the do-it-yourself aspect. Because wildlife ponds need not be especially deep or elaborately manicured, they're inexpensive to create. In many instances a waterfowl pond can be built by simply plugging a ditch or pushing up some dirt. It's encouraging to know that in the realm of environmental healing, ponds offer a low-budget solution.

A pondside wood duck box with a collar to repel predators provides waterfowl with a secure nest.

Siting

Earth ponds take shape in two basic molds: dammed or dugout. Choosing between the two is the simplest part of the pond-making process. The form is implicit in the site. To dam or to dig? The land reveals the answer.

The ideal site for a dammed pond is a wet hollow lying between two steep banks close together. Such sites are often found at the headwaters of small springs, streams, or watercourses that are dry part of the year. An earth dam can be built across the water between the banks using fill trucked to the site. But the pond maker must be careful to avoid building an earth dam across a stream that runs year-round, or that drains a large watershed, unless a major engineering project can be supported, with state approval. Besides, with fill and trucking costs rising every day, a small pond dammed with imported earth costs as much as a big one used to.

Most favored today in rolling terrain is the dug-and-dammed pond, built where excavation of the pond basin will yield enough earth for the embankment. The dug-and-dammed pond is the most efficient building style in hill country. Earth is excavated from the site, simultaneously hollowing out the pond basin and providing fill to build the dam.

On flat terrain where the water table is close to the ground, or where a nearby stream or well can be turned in, a dugout pond works best. With a shovel, backhoe, bulldozer, or dragline, the builder carves out a hole in the earth and the pond fills. A small dugout can be excavated in a day or two. The water source may be runoff, ground springs, stream diversion, piped well water, or even roof catch. Where the earth is too porous to hold water, some dugout makers lay in a liner of plastic, or clay. Steer away from so-called liquid sealers, which often don't work.

The Site

More than simply choosing a pond site, the pond maker must discover where earth and water can be joined to give birth to a reservoir. You may have a notion of a pond site, perhaps a swampy hollow that catches hillside runoff, or land close by springs or a stream. There's no substitute for native instinct. If your kinship with the land is close, you will sense where the water veins run and not misread a rush of snowmelt for a steady spring.

But to develop that instinct takes time. How does the pond maker who has been on the land only a few seasons substitute an objective system of pond siting for divine intuition?

The surest pond augur is a watershed portrait top to bottom. Every square foot of land that funnels precipitation and ground water to the pond site will affect the potential volume and water quality of the reservoir. Is the water pouring through your terrain rich enough to fill a pond? Will the basin hold water? Lacking these elements, no one can bring a pond from the earth.

Watch how rainfall runs from the highest point of your watershed to its lowest boundaries. Does runoff gather suggestively in a marsh? Might a running stream or spring be channeled to a pond site? Do springs and streams hold up during summer parches? What kind of subterranean foundation runs under your watershed and pond site? Ex-

amination of the earth's anatomy is the beginning of good pond making.

On the way to finding a pond site, certain maps and charts offer guides. U.S. Geological Survey topographic maps detail contours and waterways. Topo maps come in two scales, the 15- and 7½-inch series. Preferable is the larger-scale, more detailed, 7½-inch map. These maps help with acreage calculations essential to estimating watershed runoff and thus a fitting pond size. Often the maps are stocked by bookstores or sporting outfitters. Otherwise write to the U.S. Geological Survey Maps, Map Distribution Branch, Box 25286, Denver Federal Center, Denver, CO 80225. Ask for the USGS Index Map of your state. From this index you can determine which quadrangle covers your terrain.

Aerial photographs in two forms are available at your district Soil Conservation Service office. Conservation plan maps are aerial shots that cover about one square mile: roads, buildings, lakes, ponds, waterways, and ground cover show up. Stereoscopic aerial photographs give 3-D visions of your watershed. By tracing a planimeter over the contoured stereo image, your SCS agent can measure the boundaries of land that drain to the pond site, calculate watershed acreage, and recommend pond size.

Soil survey interpretations from the SCS office provide another source of watershed information. These interpretations include recommendations on reservoirs and embankments as well as the potential for wildlife, crops, and trees. Without digging a scoop of dirt, the pond maker can assemble these maps, photographs, and data to make a first estimate of pond prospects.

The Law

Once a rough determination of location and pond size is made, it's time to check into pond building regulations. Check with your state Water Resources Board before beginning excavation to be sure your project complies with wetland protection legislation and other construction guidelines. Local zoning laws also may affect pond construction; check with your municipal government regarding excavation. The federal government has jurisdiction over some wetlands and may require permits for pond excavation. Finally, double-check to be sure that you hold legal title to the land. I've seen pond projects held up because of property line and right-of-way disputes, and power company easements.

Soil Tests

Several times I've stood with a pond maker who neglected soil tests, gazing into a dry crater. It's a sorry sight—and a reminder that in excessively porous soil an earth pond will not hold water. Naturally, all earth ponds seep; the good ones keep it to a minimum.

Ideally soil is tested in late summer or fall, before the rains. Spring testing results in overestimates of runoff and impermeability. Begin probing potential sites with a soil auger. This steel bit gets into the earth to test for rock, ledge, and soil quality. Your Soil Conservation Service agent is available for this chore, but ponds may be low priority on his list. Why wait? Work it out for yourself. Borrow or rent an auger if you don't want to buy one. Make soil borings over each pond site being considered. If you consistently hit rock at a uniform level, it's probably ledge. Ledge or bedrock may lie deep enough to permit excavation of a pond, but fissures in the rock will drain water, especially down vertical grain. Since vigorous springs often surface in ledgey areas, the careful pond maker will site downhill from the spring, not astride it.

A good pond site will permit borings to a depth of four to eight feet. To determine soil quality, unscrew the auger from the earth and examine the material extracted at the tip. Coarse-textured sands and sand-gravel blends are extremely porous and will not hold water. Watertight clay, silty clay, and sandy clay soils make excellent pond materials. Test the soil by compressing a handful into a ball. A good clay or silty clay will hold together in a moist lump of fine textured earth.

Another method of estimating soil imperviousness is to measure the proportion of sand, silt, and clay in a sample of earth. You will need a large jar with vertical sides; a half-gallon orange juice bottle works well. Filter a soil sample through a half-inch screen, removing pebbles and gravel. Fill the jar one-third full with the soil sample, top off with water, and cap. Shake it up and then set aside for twenty-four hours. The coarse sandy material will settle first, then silt, and finally clay. The best reservoir material consists of particles ranging from small gravel or coarse sand to fine sand and clay. Measure the proportions of sand, silt, and clay. The top stratum of clay should comprise at least 20 percent.

Favorable soil samples combined with indications of ledge-free earth cue the next step in pond siting: test pits. You will want to hire a backhoe, unless you plan to dig a number of eight- to ten-foot-deep pits by hand. Again, the best season for these tests is the dry spell prior to autumn rains. Dry season excavation minimizes chances of the backhoe wasting time and money by getting mired in the mud or ripping up soggy turf. Shop around for a skillful backhoe operator, preferably with pond-making experience. Be sure your site presents no obstructions to the backhoe—no transmission wires over the pond site to snare construction equipment, no electric lines over or underground, and no pipes.

If you must cut a path to give the backhoe access to the site, be sure to clear ground around each test pit so the machine can heap soil on the downstream side of each digging. Otherwise, rain will wash earth back into the pit. A chain saw is handy on a brushy site, especially if the pit sites are picked on the spot.

Before beginning test pit excavation, stake out the approximate pond shoreline. On level ground, where a dugout pond is filling, it's simple to mark the imaginary shoreline. On sloping terrain, suited to a dug-and-dammed pond, it helps to visualize the shoreline by standing at the lowest edge of the pond area—the location of the dam—so that your eyes are in a plane with the desired water level. Remember that you want a minimum of about five to six feet of water in the pond. At this time, a hand-sighting level or transit aids the process. Inexpensive sighting levels are available at Army-Navy outfits or sport suppliers. In a pinch use a poor man's transit: set up a carpenter's level on a stepladder leveled at the shoreline height. Sight down the edge and swing the level around, following the waterline. As you mark the shore you may need to clear brush with an ax or a chain saw. Do not leave sharp stumps that could later puncture the backhoe tires.

The backhoe is the pond maker's bionic arm. In an hour or so you can unearth just about all there is to know about a pond, short of digging it. If the site fails the pit tests, it's simple to refill the holes. Skip the testing and you may wind up refilling the whole pond. Test holes should be excavated at random from the center of the pond basin to the shoreline. If the soil in the pond site seems uniform, three or four pits may be sufficient. The greater the terrain varies, the more test pits should be dug. For dammed ponds, don't forget to dig where the dam will be constructed. If the auger or the backhoe hits shallow ledge, reposition the dam or move the

pond. Dams on ledge like to unplug ponds.

As the backhoe digs, watch the earth being wormed out of the ground. You will see layers of earth: the soil "profile." The backhoe should separate the top six to eight inches of topsoil from the rest of the material. Later, this rich topsoil can nourish your shoreland. Up next is the subsoil. If you hit deep heavy soil thick with clay, you have pond maker's gold. In the northeast area of the country, where clay-rich podzol soils are common, there's plenty of opportunity to strike it rich. Beware of limestone and sandstone, too permeable to hold water.

Watch for water while the backhoe cuts into the ground. If the vein is strong, water will quickly break through the punctured earth and bleed into the test pit. On flat terrain the test pit will eventually fill to the level of your water table. Such a pit is virtually a miniature dugout pond. Its water level will be the same as that of the finished pond; additional excavation will simply enlarge the storage capacity.

So far, test pits have steered you away from ledge and shale and helped meter soil and water. If you tapped clay-rich soil and a good flow of water, you have a pond site. At this point it helps to refine the pond shoreline. Using the test pits as guides, restake the pond to exclude ledge or unsuitably porous terrain. Maximize space where water is abundant. On a sloping site where a dammed pond is planned, be sure to reserve space about thirty feet wide on the downstream shoreline for dam construction.

Storage Capacity

Now your pond can be evaluated for storage capacity. Knowing a pond's potential water volume enables you to mesh the pond size with the watershed, and thus determine the pond's potential for auxiliary use: irrigation, hydro-power, aquaculture, and fire protection. The storage capacity of a pond is usually counted in acre-feet, 325,851 gallons per acre-foot. To reckon acre-footage, first compute the surface area of the pond. At regular intervals, measure the width and length of the staked shoreline. Plot the shoreline on graph paper and add up the squares to figure surface acreage. One acre is 43,560 square feet. Next estimate the maximum water depth and multiply by 0.4. The result, multiplied by surface acreage, yields acre-footage. For instance, a pond of one-half acre with a maximum depth of ten feet holds two acre-feet, or 651,702 gallons. (The acre-footage formula averages the depth of all ponds at a uniform 40 percent of maximum.)

Knowing the storage capacity of the pond site, along with the size of the watershed, enables you to forecast reservoir-runoff compatibility. If you haven't figured your watershed size using SCS maps and photographs, mark the pond site on an USGS quadrangle map. Trace the contours of the area that drains into the site. With the 7½-inch scale, each ¼-inch square on the map represents ten acres of land; with the 15-inch, each ¼-inch square is forty acres.

In the prime pond-making country east of the Mississippi and in the northwest, this rough rule of thumb determines the ratio of watershed acreage/ground cover to pond capacity: each acre-foot of pond should receive runoff from territory no larger than two acres, if the ground cover is all woods or brush. If the ground cover is pasture, the drainage area should not exceed 1.5 acres for each acre of pond. If the drainage area is cultivated land, each acre-foot should receive runoff from no more than one acre. If the watershed is mixed, reckon accordingly.

Natural ponds form without need of formulas, of course. All these figures are approximations. I have had success overloading a pond with ten times more runoff than indicated. Overloading helps keep the pond fresh and full. But it won't work without tight watershed soils, a sturdy spillway, and, in the case of dammed ponds, a hefty embankment. By far the worse mismatch occurs where the watershed falls short of supplying the pond. It's worth a few hours of mapping and math to make sure the pond site won't leave you dry.

Water For Crops & Livestock

Calculating your pond's storage potential helps determine its capacity for watering livestock and crops.

How much water will you need for irrigation? Water requirements vary with locale, soil condition, and crop, but a healthy ration of rain usually ranges from one to two inches of water per week through the principal growing season. That translates into about 28,000 gallons of water per acre, or 600 gallons for every 1,000 square feet. A one acre-foot pond is likely to supply enough water to maintain this liquid diet without depleting the pond or bothering

fish. Larger irrigation schemes that tap 10 percent or more of the pond volume require a steady resupply of water. To be sure that the inflow is adequate, dam up your spring, pipe the inflow into a bucket, and clock the time that it takes to fill. For instance, if a five-gallon bucket fills in two minutes, your pond will take in 25,200 gallons a week, regardless of precipitation. That's enough to keep a good-sized garden and pond well watered. If your pond is already built, measure the overflow to calculate surplus. Either way, do your figuring during drought season, when irrigation will be most needed and springs low.

A pond can be tapped for irrigation in many ways. A manual or motorized pump can move water to a storage container near the garden for manual watering or, better still, above the garden on a slope or platform, for gravity-feed delivery. The pond can be the source for spraying, either motorized or manual. Backpack spray tanks designed for fertilizing, crop spraying, or firefighting make fine watering devices. Small wind pumps will move thirty gallons per hour in winds over seven mph; the Sparco windmill, for example, lifts water thirteen feet over a horizontal distance of thirty feet. If the pond lies below the garden, with sufficient additional slope further below, hydraulic rams will deliver irrigation running on waterpower.

Drip irrigation is the most conservative watering technique. Water is piped to the edge of the garden, with a shut-off valve coupled where the drip system begins. By minimizing losses to vaporization, runoff, and deep seepage, a drip system cuts in half the water required for irrigation. The most conservative use of the drip system results from small daily waterings. However, weekly irrigation encourages root growth and produces the strongest plants. One way or the other, avoid drenching crops to conserve minerals and nitrogen.

Besides supplying irrigation for gardens and orchards, a pond often creates a paddy in the spillway area that will support crops with heavy thirsts, like celery and watercress.

Livestock Water

To get an idea of your animal watering potential, balance storage capacity against needs.

Livestock Water Consumption

Cattle	9 to 18 gallons per day
Dairy Cows	8 gallons per day plus ⅓ gallon for every pound of milk given. Up to 35 gallons per cow for drinking and barn needs.
Horse or Mule	8 to 12 gallons per day
Sheep	1 to 3 gallons per day.
Laying Hens	8 gallons per day, per hundred
Turkeys	10 to 15 gallons per day, per hundred
Rabbits	1 gallon per day, per dozen
Pig	1 to 3 gallons per day.

Ponds intended exclusively for livestock should be available in each pasture or grazing field, spaced about a quarter-mile apart in rough terrain, and no more than one mile apart in level areas. This spacing encourages uniform grazing. Ponds designed for both stock watering and recreation should be fenced so that the shoreline will not be trampled and the water muddied. The pond can be fenced completely, and stock water delivered by gravity pressure or pump. Otherwise, the pond can be partially enclosed, leaving a small area of the shore open to animals. Limited access works best in ponds with earth spillways. The access is located close to the outlet channel, so the current naturally flushes mud and manure from the pond. This system works best for waterfowl, chickens, and other lightweight critters. Heavier stock can quickly shred the turf and clog drainage ditches, especially during wet weather. Ponds intended exclusively for stock need not be expensive. In a few hours, a backhoe can excavate a small dugout that makes a fine waterhole or a habitat for waterfowl.

Excavation

Before machines lightened the work of clearing and excavating, stream impoundments were the most popular man-made reservoirs. The shore was simply skinned at the waterline where the dam would be notched into the banks. Later, excavated ponds were built with animals pulling plows, harrows, scrapers, and stumps. Labor was kept to a minimum by careful selection of terrain. Sites were chosen in open hollows with tight soil and good water prospects, where a minimum of stump removal and deep digging was needed. If the excavated earth could be used to build the dam, the site was considered especially promising. Trees that had to be removed were chopped and cleared from the area, roots and all. Sometimes cleared brush was piled aside, later to be heaped along the shoreline of the embankment, cinched in by a submerged fence. These brush liners were thought to prevent erosion along new dams whipped by choppy water.

After the pond maker had cleared the site, he brought in horse-drawn plows to carve up slabs of sod throughout the basin. These were saved to be grafted later to the raw land around the pond. Then the site was harrowed and scraped to hollow it out.

If an earth dam was planned, the foundation was carefully prepared to ensure a seamless bond between the foundation ground and the earthfill embankment. A center line ditch was plowed out, topped with a foot or two of impervious soil, and packed by tramping animals. The ditch was then filled with a foot or two of earth and packed again.

Most pond makers shunned bedrock foundations because of the difficulty of creating a watertight seal between stone and earth. But given the choice of a ledge-based dam or no pond at all, stubborn pond makers scraped the earth off the rock and carved a one-foot notch down the dam's base center line. The notch was covered with a reinforced cement wall, one or two feet high. On top of that the dam was raised. As the embankment was mounded and packed, supply pipes for barn or household water were laid in at levels below the frost line and covered with earth. Then draft animals were led around the excavation, tramping and packing.

This was doubly effective when coordinated with rising pond water. As the basin filled, the animals were led in a spiral around the ascending waterline, packing it tight. This concluding step spanned the period it took the pond to fill, often several weeks.

If the basin material was not naturally watertight, hay was spread around the reservoir and tramped in. Manure might then be added and packed in to help tighten the seal. Sometimes grass was seeded in the unfilled pond, and a herd of animals turned in to graze. The basin developed a watertight glaze under their hooves. The pond maker who had set aside slabs of sod had several options when the excavation was complete. He could graft the turf onto the basin whenever the earth was too porous, or onto the embankment to prevent erosion. Sod was especially desirable along the leeward waterline of a large pond exposed to strong winds. To prevent erosion at the waterline, pond makers often lapped the sod shingle fashion. A word of caution: These traditional scaling techniques nourished warmwater fish ponds, but large doses of manure and organic matter didn't help trout.

Machines

The current popularity of ponds is due largely to big earth-moving machines. Hydraulic power speeds excavation, of course; but it's the tracks and tremendous weight that add the finishing touch—super-tight compaction of the basin and dam.

As the form of the pond varies, so does the pond-making machine. Big dugouts in wet terrain are usually scooped out by dragline excavator. Smaller dugouts can be built with a dragline or backhoe. Most dugouts require backup support from a bulldozer to spread and pack the earth. Dammed ponds often can be built from start to finish with a single bulldozer.

Dugouts

The place to learn the basics of pond excavation is in a dugout. The principles of construction are primitive: for every scoop of earth removed you get a scoop of water, and there are no dams to build. As one contractor told me, "Dugouts? Hell, you can build them just about anyway you please!"

Because every gallon of water must be gained by excavation, big dugouts get expensive. But a modest one can be carved in a few days, or a few hours. Small-scale dugouts make thrifty fish ponds and greenhouse heat sinks.

Dugouts are popular with commercial fish farmers who grow warmwater fish in the South and Midwest, where clusters of small dugouts can be better managed than one big pond. In the grain belt, farmers are beginning to carve fields into dugouts, where they produce fish more efficiently than corn or wheat. Cattlemen in the West excavate dugouts to make waterholes for ranging stock. Dugouts can be carved deep, with a small surface area, to conserve water more efficiently than shallower embankment ponds—an ad-

vantage where evaporation is a problem.

A dugout can be supplied with water in two ways. The simplest arrangement is to site the pond in a broad drainage way where it will fill naturally. Otherwise, offset dugouts are carved near a water source, preferably downhill; water is channeled in by a pipe or a ditch. The source may be anything from well water to runoff from a roof catch.

Earth is the main crop of dugout excavation. Usually the earth is spread over the land bordering the pond. A garden or a beach can be landscaped around the northern shore of the pond to catch lots of sunlight. Be careful to keep garden manure from leaching into the pond, unless you plan to raise a crop of algae for warmwater fish; trout do not appreciate a pond full of plankton.

I watched the earth from one large dugout spread over surrounding swampland to make a hayfield. As the basin was excavated, a dragline dumped earth into trucks that shuttled back and forth from the emerging field. When the dugout pond was done, three acres of fertile ground surrounded it.

To achieve tight adhesion between the surface and the new terrain, the land should first be prepared by removing roots and large stones. Some pond makers plow and harrow before applying fill. Others remove the topsoil completely with a bulldozer. Often the excavated earth from a dugout is used to build barriers to deflect water, wind, or snow. For instance, barn runoff or silty ground flow can be channeled away from a pond with a berm or a gutter of earth built from the excavated diggings. Cattle waterholes on western rangelands are built to stand protected in the lee of earth mounds that deflect snow and wind. These deflectors are built about ten feet back from the pond shore to prevent crushing of the banks, with gradual slopes to prevent slumping. Earth heaps of any kind should not be built

just upstream from the dugout, where they can wash into the pond.

Although a dugout can be excavated in wet terrain by dragline, the diggings may be too wet to spread immediately. Some dugout builders prefer to muck out wet sites in the fall and let the earth dry over the winter. The pond is finished off the following spring. For finish grading, the best landscaping tool is a lightweight dozer.

While landscaping the dugout, be sure not to elevate the banks more than three or four feet high. Too much rim around the pond creates a crater and invites erosion and trouble with access. Keep in mind that fill will settle. Earth that is dozer-packed may settle up to 5 percent of its depth; unpacked, it may settle as much as 10 percent.

Excavation

Once your dugout site is cleared, stake the pond at intervals of fifty feet or less. Check with a level to make sure the dugout basin is on an even footing. There should be no more than a foot or two of slope. Otherwise, excavation will create enormous banks on the upstream end. No matter how hard you try, water will not tilt. A sloping site calls for an embankment pond, not a dugout.

Look over the staked pond site and satisfy yourself that the dugout is not boxed in too tightly by the terrain. In a rich watershed you may want to enlarge the pond later, or add additional ones. Supplementary dugouts sometimes are excavated near a large pond; a small downstream dugout makes a good habitat for waterfowl and warmwater fish, critters that you may not want in the main pond. Upstream dugouts can be used to settle sediment before it flows into the main pond.

When you are satisfied with the shape, size, and position of the dugout, mark the shoreline stakes with the depth of excavation and the angle of the basin slopes to guide your equipment operator. The deeper the dugout, the greater the storage capacity, the longer the life span, and the higher the price. Minimum depth is about four to five feet. Shallower, it is likely to sprout weeds and freeze fish. However, shallow dugouts can be used for aquadomes, sauna baths, fire ponds, irrigation, livestock water, etc.

Dugout banks can be cut at a rather steep angle, about 2:1, because there is no dam to slump—and because draglines and backhoes cut a steeper wall than a bulldozer. Steep banks increase storage space and discourage weeds. Do not cut the slopes any steeper than 2:1 unless you reinforce the basin. In fact, you might want to grade one bank at a gradual 3:1 or 4:1 slope to make a beach or a ramp for watering animals.

Contractors

Booking an earth-moving machine is like booking a fishing trip: it's the captain's ship but your charter. Choose an experienced contractor you trust, with equipment that suits your plans and budget. Don't let the intimidating roar of the bulldozer drown out your questions or suggestions.

If you are planning to build a small dugout, a backhoe makes a thrifty precision digger. This hydraulic scoop is about the cheapest power shovel available. Because of its short reach, the backhoe is most efficient at carving ponds ten to twenty feet in diameter or long, narrow lagoons or raceways.

A circular dugout of larger storage capacity requires larger equipment. In a site that is not swamped, the best all-around machine is a bulldozer. Unlike other heavy equipment, a bulldozer is capable of making a pond from start to finish: clearing topsoil, cuffing out rocks and roots, carving the basin, installing pipe, and spreading earth over

the shore. Bulldozers can excavate up to 1,200 cubic yards of earth in a day.

If the basin is badly drenched, the earth will be too heavy for the machine to move. All the horsepower in the world is worthless if the machine sinks, so timing is a critical factor. The best bet for success with a bulldozer in a dugout is during the driest season of the year, in a site flanking the main flow of water, to be fed by side pipe or a ditch.

To keep the basin drained during excavation, pond builders sometimes dig a ditch leading out of the downstream area of the basin or bail out water with a pump, or both. This can put a hole in your budget because it may double excavation time and cost for the machinery.

Where drainage problems threaten to swamp the bulldozer and your budget, the dragline is the best tool for a dugout. The dragline succeeds where bulldozers disappear because it works from outside the pond basin, perched on solid ground or a portable platform of planks or steel. A dragline can yank out roots and stones, scrape ledge clean, hoist pipe, and dredge soggy earth. This makes it ideal for restoring old ponds as well as digging fresh ones. However, a dragline cannot efficiently clear topsoil, pack a pond basin, or grade landscape.

The dragline operator usually begins a dugout by digging a ditch through the middle of the site to drain water. Then, working from the middle of the basin back to the shoreline, he scoops out the earth and dumps it on the banks to dry and later to be spread on the landscape.

In theory, a dragline could build a pond of unlimited size by moving back earth from the site continuously, but the cost of handling the earth over and over again grows with the size of the pond. With its reach of about forty-five feet, the dragline can most practically dig a pond about ninety feet wide. On larger dugouts a bulldozer must accompany the dragline to help with earth removal. A dragline can excavate roughly 900 yards of earth a day.

Dug-and-Dammed Ponds

Sloping terrain makes dugout excavation impractical, so pond makers build embankments of earth to hold water. By raising a dam on a hill, across a draw, or around the downstream end of a sloping hollow, the builder fills in the missing rim of an earth bowl. When the dam tops the level of the planned upstream shoreline, the pond is complete.

The amount of excavation needed to create a dug-and-dammed pond will vary depending on the terrain and the storage capacity desired. In a good pond site—a sloping hollow—excavation and embankment construction should be swift. If the pond site is on a steep hill that lacks natural enclosing flanks, substantial yardage must be dug from the basin and moved to the embankment. A neighbor had to carve a sixteen-foot deep pond because he needed so much earth to complete his dam. The earth from my eight-foot deep pond, on a more gradual slope, provided enough fill to complete my dam.

Since the upstream slope of the pond site contributes roughly half of the bowl at the outset, the pond maker must complete the enclosure by raising the rim around the lower end. A veteran pond maker will often plan the dam in his head, tramping around the site and eyeballing the slope, and then build the pond without pounding a single stake. On the other hand, Soil Conservation Service agents usually stake the site, calculate elevations every fifty feet, and draw up scale models of the pond, dam, and surrounding terrain. I think it's best to compromise: plan the dam with a few dozen stakes and a transit or level.

Site the dam first by setting up a transit or a level inside the pond basin. Level it at about two feet above the desired

upstream shoreline, giving you the necessary freeboard. Now swing the sight downstream until the land first drops out of view, and mark the spot. There the dam will butt into the slope. Continue to sight across the downstream end of the pond, tracing the top of your imaginary dam, until you again sight land. Mark the spot. Now you have fixed the two points where the embankment will tie into the land. Between these marks you will build the dam.

You may want an embankment that runs fairly straight across the slope or one that curves. On a steep slope it may prove too costly to run the dam out very far. But on a gradual slope you may be able to impound a large reservoir with a long, curving, shallow dam. The difference in elevation across the pond site determines the height of the dam. For example, if the downstream edge of the site lies six feet below the upstream shoreline and you add a couple of feet for freeboard, an eight-foot dam is required.

Foundation work for the dam involves clearing topsoil, boulders, and stumps from the dam base area. The earth beneath the dam must be tested to judge its ability to fulfill its double function: holding up the dam structure and holding in the water. Test pits in the embankment area will enable you to judge the quality of the ground base. The best ground base is a mixture of watertight clays and silts, with some sand and gravel. Bedrock or ledge in the base area may contain water-draining fissures and prevent a good seal between the ground and the dam, and should be avoided.

Ground with an excess of sand and gravel makes poor material for the dam base. Pond makers in Vermont often remedy sandy sites by digging a center-line core trench in the dam base and packing it with watertight clay-rich soil, carved from the pond basin or elsewhere. This trench is cut three to six feet wide and one to two feet deep. If the pond maker can dig through the sand into a clay or silt layer, so much the better. After the watertight material is packed into the core trench, the embankment is raised.

A swampy base of silt and clay also requires special foundation work. Clay and silt hold water, but in excess make a weak base, which can cause the dam to slump. This is remedied by enlarging the base of the foundation and flattening the embankment slopes inside and out.

The dam for my pond was based on swampy clay and silt, so it was built sixty feet wide at the base and twenty feet wide on the top. That helped distribute the load over a large area. In some swampy dam sites, pond makers cut core trenches similar to those used in sandy sites. Spongy organic material is removed and replaced with a clay-silt-sand mixture or concrete.

A basin that consists of good impervious pond material will usually yield earthfill satisfactory for the dam itself. Material containing about 20 percent clay, without too much sand, gravel, or organic matter, is best. An excess of either sand-gravel or silt-clay will weaken the dam. Where sand and gravel make up a large portion of the earthfill, pond makers build a core of clay-rich earth throughout the dam to prevent leakage. Clay-rich material can sometimes be scooped up from select areas of the excavation for this inner core. To help waterproof the dam, the embankment is built wide, with 2:1 slopes. Pond makers caution against using embankment fill composed of organic silt or pure clay. These materials hold water, but they make poor dam material. The organic matter will decompose, while the clay is liable to dry and crack.

When the makeup of the foundation base and the earthfill has been determined, you can choose your dam location and stake it out. Begin by staking out the center line of the dam every twenty-five feet or so, using markers tall enough

to top the dam surface. Peg the inside and outside lines of the dam to completely trace the base size. Using the recommended 2:1 slope, a ten-foot-wide embankment with a ten-foot wide top surface—just big enough for tractors, trucks, and barbecues—needs a fifty-foot base, so lines pegged about twenty-five feet on either side of the center line mark its foundation.

Once you see the rough shape of the dam you can consider the spillway site. The spillway should be located where it can exhaust water directly over the top of the dam and down into a suitable water channel, already established by ground-water flow. You don't want to run overflow down your driveway or straight into your garden. The spillway area of the dam is one place you don't skimp: it must be tough. Spillways are often placed on the seam where the dam ties into the natural terrain. (See Spillways.)

The natural flow of the bulldozer is downhill, scooping up earth and pushing it across the site to the dam. Sometimes topsoil and debris are pushed to the extreme edge of the embankment foundation and buried under the rising dam. This organic material must be built into the far outside of the core structure of the dam, where it can decay without opening up leaks. Large boulders should be excluded from the embankment. They may be pushed off to the flanks of the site and later retrieved for diving headstones and fish shelters. As the excavation deepens, water will begin to flow into the basin. If pooling water threatens to bog down the machine, a drainage ditch may be required. The builder's final task will be to put in the plug by filling the ditch.

Spillways

The Perils of Piping

The new thirst for ponds reminds me of the beginning of the wood-heat renaissance a generation ago: lots of trial and error. Pond makers today are chalking up mistakes at about the same rate that wood burners did. Most of the wasted time and money is going down the drain through underground spillways. It's time for land users to take a new look at the open sesame of pondmaking: piping.

Some background first. Earth ponds flow naturally toward oblivion. Vegetation decays, sediment accumulates, and the basin erodes. Eventually, without help, the pond disappears. Pond keepers resist decay in several ways. Inflows of water are maintained to reduce silt and sediment. Unwanted aquatic growth is discouraged with deep-dug, steep-sided basins and annual drawdowns. And the reservoir is designed to withstand the abrasive force of overflowing water. It is this effort to exhaust overflow without damaging the earth structure that constitutes the main line of defense.

I recently revisited a couple of ponds that I watched being carved last year, one in New Hampshire and one in Vermont. Both had been sited to catch ample runoff and spring water. Both were sidehill dug-and-dammed ponds. And both covered about a quarter-acre surface, plunging to ten feet at the deepest. In fact, these two ponds mirrored each other across the Connecticut River, with one big difference: the New Hampshire pond was fitted with an underground drain coupled to a standpipe, while the Vermont pond was designed to expel surplus water over a simple spillway across the embankment. Two steady streams of water leaked from the New Hampshire pond, one through the tar-covered eight-inch corrugated steel drain, the other seeping out just beneath the pipe. Its water level was three feet below the standpipe opening, despite rich spring rains that had saturated the earth and topped off neighboring ponds. In Vermont, the simpler earth pond brimmed full. Surplus water overflowed smoothly down the riprap-lined channel. No piping, no leaks. The excavation price for each pond was a modest $2000; but with the addition of pipe, the total for the New Hampshire pond had risen substantially.

"What's the price of pipe now?" I asked Leonard Cook, a Norwich, Vermont, pond builder. He laughed. "No one knows! It changes everyday!" But he guessed that the materials for the T-riser system in the New Hampshire pond had added another $1000 to the cost. And it leaked.

Despite the pitfalls, it's not hard to fathom the lure of pond plumbing, especially in embankment ponds. A bottom drain offers the potential for kitchen-faucet control of the reservoir: fast flushing for fish harvests and repairs, and push-button drawdowns to quell unwanted shoreline growth. And some say that winter fishkills in north-country ponds can be stopped by piping out the lower layer of water, which may grow fatally oxygen-lean under ice and snow. Add a standpipe to the underground drain and the pond keeper's mastery seems complete; a vertical pipe lopped off at the desired level promises to maintain a steady water-line—*if* the incoming water is sufficient. And in small ponds fed by mammoth watersheds, heavy overflow through a standpipe may be preferable to stressing an overland spill-

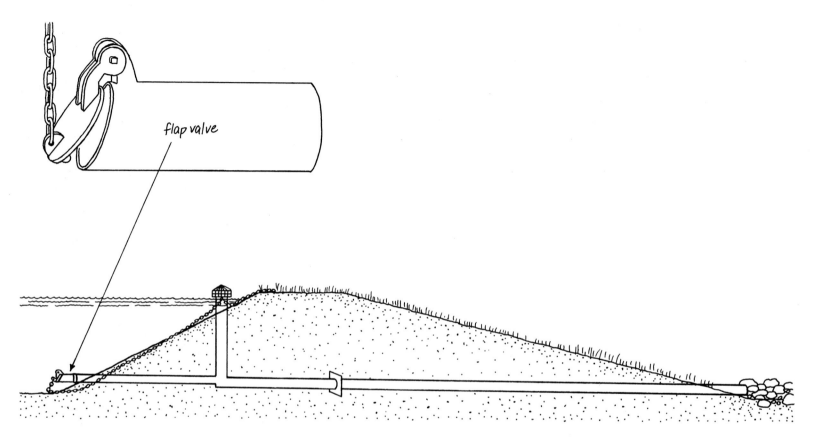

flap valve

This drop-inlet pipe spillway with drainpipe can be used to maintain a specific pond level as well as to drain it. On plastic pipe drains, a cap with a screw eye is often installed. A chain or cable attached to the screw eye is hooked to the top of the drop-inlet for access. Once the cap is pulled, the pond drains completely. Controlled draining can be accomplished by using a flap valve, also controlled by a chain (see inset). Ball valves are sometimes installed in the drainpipe with access by a valve well, but the fitting is quite expensive. Note that the drain pipe is smaller than the drop-inlet. This reduces flow during draining, preventing downstream erosion. Trash racks are optional; if used they should be monitored regularly to prevent clogging and subsequent flooding.

A common leakage problem occurs along a pond's drainpipe. During construction of the dam, when the pipe is installed, the fill should be compacted around the pipe. An anti-seep collar (or two if the dam is more than fifteen feet high) should be placed around the pipe. Reinforced concrete collars, six inches or more thick, are often used with concrete, asbestos-cement, and cast iron pipe, and plastic diaphragms can be used with plastic pipe. Exterior grade plywood anti-seep collars are not recommended; they rot.

way. Yet, like the New Hampshire pond keeper who is having his pipe system sealed with concrete and replaced by an embankment spillway, many people find themselves badly served by subterranean plumbing.

How come? The basic problem is poor design integrity. Earth and steel don't mix. The whole system is aching to leak, and the pond maker's first occasion to use the drain is usually to fix it. Easier said than done. The drain plug probably lies buried in sediment at the bottom of the pond. The plug is often no more than a simple softwood stopper hewed and stuffed into the underwater end of the pipe, and the uncorking action is a strong punch with a long pipe applied from the outside. Of course, once the plug is smashed out, there's no closing it. So much for push-button

control. The notion of maintaining a perfect water level is often another fantasy. In many ponds the standpipe pokes up like the periscope on a stray submarine because the inflow is not rich enough to produce a constant surplus. Or, even more likely, because the pipe leaks.

Usually two kinds of drain pipe are favored: culvert-style steel or iron. Steel pipe is available in lengths that can be trucked to the pond site and then bolted together. Yet, unless pond makers are careful to use tar-coated, double-riveted spiral pipe, spot-welded in the trench, they may soon find a leak squirting through the seams. Iron pipe from a scrapyard is thriftier. But because several pieces usually must be welded together to gain sufficient length, careful installation is crucial. Without a solid base and good

The inside slope of a pond can be as steep as 2:1, if the soil is stable enough to remain firm. A 3:1 slope is far more common, and 4:1 is used for swimming and livestock watering slopes.

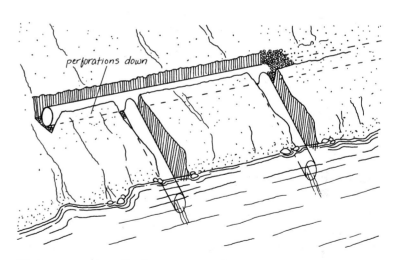

To prevent erosion of a slope upstream from a pond, dig a ditch across the slope parallel to the pond and install perforated pipe with outlets carrying seepage into the pond. Fill the ditch with crushed stone. An optional vertical T at the upstream end of the main pipe allows for occasional flushing to remove sediment.

85

earth packing, settling movements can break the joints. If an overflow standpipe is coupled to the drain, the drainpipe must be tilted slightly downward to get a clean flow and to prevent sediment from clogging the way. Eight- to twelve-inch stock is favored for small ponds.

Siting the drain is tricky. Pond makers must anticipate the main inflow of water and locate the pipe safely beyond the turbulence. I saw one job take a costly detour when the drainage ditch had to be refilled and carved in a new location because the main vein of spring water splashed too close to the planned outlet. The builder knew that silt soon would bury the drain.

Most frustrating of all is the potential for leakage from a perfectly sealed drain or standpipe system. At sixty-two pounds per cubic foot, pond water has a powerful tendency to squirt out around the exterior of the buried pipe. Pond makers who install pipe overcome this by ringing the outside of the pipe with anti-seep collars. These fittings clasp tightly to the pipe like nuts on a bolt. Good pond makers shudder at the thought of installing pipe without anti-seep collars. Yet they admit that collars are no guarantee against leakage. A pipe in the pond basin is like a splinter that never goes away.

For some builders, the answer to the piping dilemma is plastic sewer pipe with built-in joint gaskets. The seal is tight, and plastic will not rust. However, the jury is still out on durability over the years.

There are instances when piping is needed. Large overflows sometimes require piping to avoid erosion. Spillways which vehicles must cross are usually piped under the road. Drain pipes allow fish farmers to harvest and clean out ponds efficiently. In some areas building codes may require spillway pipe, whether or not it's structurally necessary. Plastic, iron, or steel: pipe anti-seep collars are a must.

Earth Spillways

All this piping business is simply a prelude to earth spillways, which I find far superior to subterranean piping in ponds suitably matched to their watersheds.

A good earth spillway keeps a pond overflowing smoothly when inflow creates a surplus. Otherwise, the spillway takes a rest. No standpipe poking up in the air. No seeps. For a pond that overflows only during heavy rains or thaws, a riprapped earth spillway near the downstream end of the pond usually is adequate. Commonsense conservation methods make the best spillway foundation: avoid erodible soils and prevent debris from clotting the channel. The greater the overflow, the tougher the spillway must be to resist erosion. In Vermont, granite slabs or stone will be found lining especially hardworking spillways. A simple grassy channel, however, can be sufficient to carry off overflow from a dugout pond. If the downstream area where the spillway will discharge has been disturbed by excavation, the vegetative cover can be reestablished while the pond fills.

The spillway for an embankment pond is carved by bulldozer (or shovel) at the conclusion of construction, deep enough to guarantee two or three feet of banking above the high-water mark. Such a spillway is often located at the end of the dam where the embankment is spliced to the natural slope. This area is a good site for the overflow since the upstream hillside provides a natural stronghold against erosion. Of the two seams where dam and hillside meet, the spillway should be laid where the overflow will best stream away without eroding the embankment structure.

Spillways are divided into three sections: the approach channel, the control section, and the exit slope. The *approach channel* is an extension of the slope of the pond basin leading out of the pond. The slope angle should be inclined back

into the pond at an angle of at least two or three degrees so that water will drain clean back into the reservoir. Good drainage means fewer mosquitos. Make the approach at least twice as wide as the control section. The *control section*, or crest, is the level channel that runs through the embankment about one to three feet below the embankment rim. This channel should be located on the upstream side of the midpoint of the embankment, anywhere from two to ten feet wide, and at least ten feet long. The longer the control section, the better its ability to handle overflow. A turn in the control section is permissible, but be sure the sweep is slow and easy. No abrupt angles. To help buffer erosion, the spillway control section should be reinforced with a riprap of stones about three inches in diameter. These may be culled from the raw new embankment or imported. Otherwise, bricks or fieldstone can be applied. I would avoid treated wood because of possible water contamina-tion. Culvert pipe—whole or cut in half lengthwise—makes an unreliable liner since water tends to work out underneath, especially after frost heaving. The banks of the spillway control section should be mulched to protect against erosion, and vegetation reestablished. Spillway side slopes should be moderate, no steeper than 3:1, to prevent slumping.

The *exit channel* should drain overflow away from the pond without damaging the downstream slope of the embankment. The exit channel will drop off at about the same angle as the outside of the dam. Like the control section, it should be lined with stones or other reinforcement and maintained with conservation tactics. Wing dikes sometimes are used to protect the embankment. Water should be carried far enough below the dam to prevent any washing back or eddying that might cause damage in a flood.

The Digger: A Stream Pond that Carves Itself

One summer I swam in a stream pond in the second curve of an oxbow in Abbott Brook. The flow had chiseled into the bank, sweeping out a twenty-foot bowl, then doubled back where the roots of a poplar grove held the bank together. Rebounding sediment had settled into a sandy beach on the shallow bank. You could swim all day against the current and never get anywhere.

This stretch of brook with its whirly-pit was one of the brightest lures when the surrounding land was deeded to a young family from California. Lee Ann and Mike turned salvage from an old carriage house into a post-and-beam saltbox near the bank and counted on the pond for household water and summer baths. One summer afternoon, with some help from their daughter Heather, they laid up a stone dam to deepen the basin to six feet. They chopped down a poplar to bridge the brook—great for hanging by the knees in the free current. But with autumn rains came a tide of silt that filled the little pond, and ice and spring snow melt crumpled the dam.

Just south, Dave and Victoria built a silo house out of dismantled Army barracks trucked from Michigan. It was a memorial to thrift and Sixties sentiment. Really monumental was their cellar sauna and front-yard pond. The sauna was about 350 cubic feet. Clear cedar boards lined the interior and two racks of slatted benches crisscrossed the room. A mail-order sheet-metal stove burned with cheery red cheeks near a knee-high window that peered over a rocky brook. During tower construction David and Tor had let the brook run loose. With the house together,

they looked around and decided to make a pond. They built a stone dam and shoveled silt out of the basin. The dam was laid up loose enough to pass the flow and contain a pool. It filled deep enough to inspire David, after a midnight sauna, to climb the ladder to his tower roof and leap for the dark pond below. But spring came with runoff that punched out the dam and swept in a load of silt—a nuisance for the rest of us and potentially fatal for David.

So a ritual grew in the summer. Neighbors gathered at different stream ponds for dam repair and silt shoveling. Given a good blend of hot sun and cold beer it was okay, until you got your toe crunched. I began to ponder a better solution. I found it in a fifteen-year-old illustrated bulletin published by the New York State Conservation Department. "The stream pond," I read, "must lie *below* the dam." It's simple geology: pools form naturally in the wake of a waterfall.

"Log pyramid pool digger" is the title the conservationists tagged their pond-making method, and it wasn't long before I saw how smoothly it worked. With my neighbors, Blake and Aletta, who live on the brink of Podunk Brook, I raised a barrier of logs and stones across the water, triggering a waterfall that carved out a pond. Now it flows like a self-propelled excavator and sweeps itself clean every spring—a sorcerer's impoundment. We just call it the *digger pond*.

A side-hill pond is a bath; the digger is a whirlpool. Stillwater ponds lie under ice half the year; the churning digger pond freezes for two or three of winter's coldest months, at most. The digger attracts native trout without trapping them, simultaneously stirring up a richly aerated pond suitable for cage-culturing fish. And it makes a fine sauna site.

As with all forms of pond making, success depends on tapping natural advantages of terrain. A stream has a way of hinting at the best site for a digger pond: a hollow that could be enlarged, a slow shallow flow between stable banks, or a pool already forming under existing falls. Banks should be at least three or four feet high, and sites prone to flooding avoided.

The size of the digger basin will be limited by the breadth of the stream, so look for a site wide enough to let you stretch out—"Ample and large, that the arms spread abroad might not be hurt," as Cicero described the ideal pond—but not so wide that finding dam materials is difficult, or where watershed runoff will overload the structure. A stream spanning ten to twenty feet, catching runoff from less than ten square miles, works well. Dam materials should be close at hand. Our digger dam was built with trees felled at the site. Round timbers about a foot in diameter make the best structure, with hemlock, cedar, and tamarack topping the list. For longest durability the bark should be peeled. Stones can be used in place of timber, although the dam will be less effective, if quicker to build.

Dams are subject to a trio of wracking forces: sliding, crushing, and overthrow. A strong foundation will prevent sliding, and a tight structure will avert crushing and overthrow. The best foundation for a digger is bedrock or solid bottom. A base of sand or mud will undermine the structure. If you fail to find a solid base it may be possible to create one using an old loggers' technique for building stream-driven dams: drive a row of wooden pilings into the stream bed to keep the bottom from washing away and to form a base to which the sills of the dam can be bolted.

To be most effective, the dam should rest on a pair of sill timbers that traverse the stream, lying flat on the bottom and butted into the banks. To ensure that the dam does not slide, an elaborate anchoring technique was suggested in the New York State bulletin. A trench is excavated about two feet wide, four feet deep into the banks, the base level with the stream bed. If stream water is high it may be diverted to one side by temporary dams made of logs or stone. Here on the Podunk, to save labor and comply with Vermont regulations against stream course alteration, we found low-water construction best.

Drift bolts are used to pin the twin timbers to the stream bed, and an additional log is entrenched about four feet upstream. The sills are then tied to this anchor log with galvanized poultry wire. The pond maker drills one-inch holes every six feet or so in parallel sills and pins down the base by sledgehammering ¾-inch concrete reinforcing bars through the logs, deep into the stream bed. Six-foot lengths of rebar sunk five feet deep leave a foot to crimp over and hold down the sills. Obstructions in the stream bed may be sidestepped by repositioning the bolts or backfilling and weighing down the butt ends of the sills. Additional drift bolts should be pinned two feet to either side of the joints. The six-inch anchor log is then entrenched about four feet upstream of the sills, flush with the stream bed, and drift-bolted or otherwise firmly secured. The chicken wire is then used to tie the sills to the anchor, as well as create a ramp to sweep water over the dam. The wire is blanketed over the width of the stream and secured to the anchor log and sills with galvanized nails or staples. Fine brush is layered over the wire and anchored with flat stones to complete the seal. Finally, two logs of similar girth are fitted into the sill crevice and spiked at the outside ends, leaving a mid-stream gap of a foot or two. The central opening is then cut wide enough to pass the entire flow of the stream into the center of the pond. This trimming should be synchronized with a run of low water. Additional spikes are added to secure the logs, with an eight-inch board nailed over the exposed sills to cleat the wire.

Of course, nothing in the world of natural stream ponds resembles such a structure. Aletta, Blake, and I didn't hesitate to assemble a simpler digger dam. We bridged the stream with a pair of balsam timbers, anchored the butts with stones, and backfilled the upstream side with more stones. By adding a rim of stones at the downstream end of the pond, Aletta made sure that even in a drought the pond spans fifteen feet with four or five feet of water.

Blake and Aletta are guaranteed a regular catch from the pond in season. And since the pond is cupped at the head of a stretch of water that flows dead south, it gathers direct and reflected sun. Blake built a sauna at the northwest end of the pond, taking advantage of the sun to supplement the sauna's wood fire. Through all but the deepest freezes the pond stays clear for sauna baths. If their household water freezes up, the digger pond holds a reservoir of emergency water.

"It looks like a backwards dammed pond," Blake said a while back, soaking under the falls between saunas. "But it sure does work."

Digger dams are often used to carve the trouble-free reservoirs for offset ponds. Here a small digger collects stream water to feed a nearby pond sited in dry terrain. Water cascading over the dam simultaneously fills the basin and sweeps sediment away from the feed pipe, which lies just beneath the surface, plugged into a cement block. The pipe runs 100 yards downhill to the offset embankment pond.

The digger dam is sloped and stepped to regulate stream flow through notches spanning the pool. Rot-resistant hemlock 4 × 4's sunk into the banks keep the flow from working around the flanks. Spanning the downstream end of the digger pool, a loose-stone dam helps contain water. The pipe is 4" PVC.

One hundred yards downhill from the digger pond lies an offset embankment pond.

1) Dig two trenches across the stream bottom and four feet into the banks. Lay two logs in the downstream trench and one in the upstream, anchored with one-fourth inch reinforcing rods. Site the trenches roughly four feet apart.

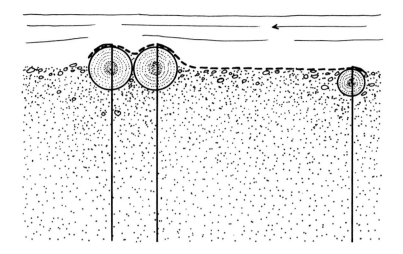

2) Lay two-inch mesh wire over the logs and stream bottom, stapled to the logs.

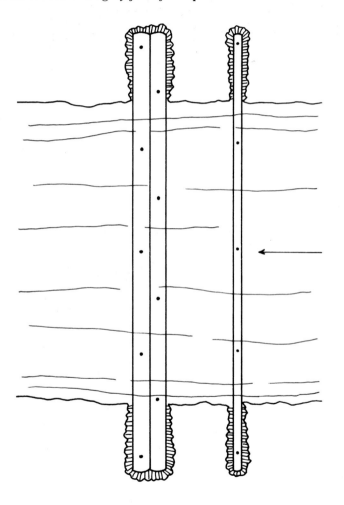

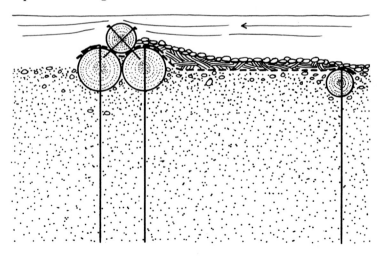

3) Spike smaller logs to the top of the downstream logs, leaving a mid-stream gap of one or two feet. Fasten only the outer ends of the top logs to the sills.

4) *Cover the wire mesh with brush and then stones. Anchor the ends with soil and rocks. Now the notch should be enlarged by cutting back on each log alternately from the center of the spillway until the entire flow of the stream passes through. This opening should be cut during an average low water period. Add spikes to secure the topside logs. Once the center opening is set, nail down an eight-inch-wide board to the two sill logs to cover the exposed wire.*

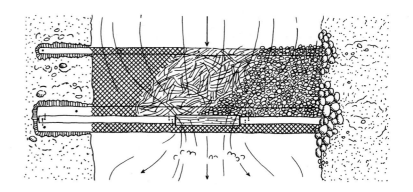

5) *The digger dam carves, cleans, and aerates the in-stream swimming hole. It will flow ice-free two or three months longer than a still water pond.*

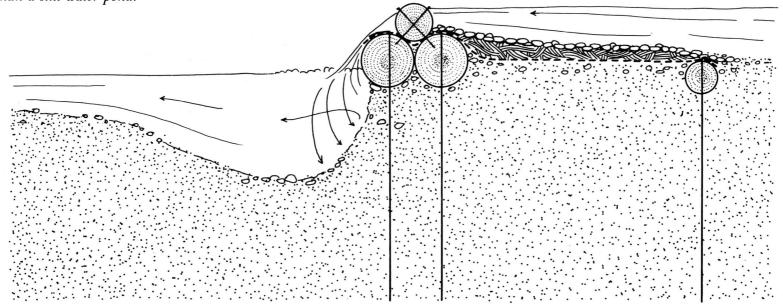

Part III
Pond Care

The Pond Keeper's Seasons
Troubleshooting Guide
Pond Repairs
Controlling Pond Weeds and Algae
Healthy Ponds Need Plenty of Fresh Air
How to Buy a Used Pond

The Pond Keeper's Seasons

"Ponds need no such labor and charges as other commodities do." That was how the elder Pliny saw the need of pond maintenance nineteen centuries ago, and it's a view that still looks good, especially to stewards of land-based labor-intensive farming schemes. To many of them, pond culture has all the lure of a forever-standing *Gone Fishin'* sign. Yet anyone who's tended a pond knows the periodic chores: erosion and weed control, spillway repair, cleanup, and most vexing, plugging leaks. The pond keeper who neglects them imperils fish, water, pond, and the neighbors downstream. If, indeed, pond culture requires less labor than most country endeavors, the reason has more to do with the pond keeper than with the pond itself—for the cunning pond keeper works with the seasons, synchronizing chores with the life cycle of the pond and tapping the forces of nature for support.

Winter

The advantages of pond keeping by the season are most dramatic in the winter. The very existence of some ponds depends on it. Across town, tucked behind the Strafford meeting house, sits a small, flat field. For more than forty summers it has been Elwin Coburn's potato patch. And every winter it is transformed. Village firemen spray down sheets of ice and create a skating pond.

It's the transformation of water into a crystalline platform that makes winter magic for pond keeping. For instance, why measure surface acreage in summer? Throwing soggy lines around the shoreland seems off the mark when it's so simple to stand on ice and pace the feet in snow.

The sand drop is another well-esteemed pond keeper's trick that takes advantage of the ice deck. It's an upkeep technique well suited to older ponds in need of restoration, particularly where aquatic vegetation or mud get unruly. To set up a sand drop, the pond keeper spreads a two-to four-inch layer of sand—*not* salted road sand—over the ice. In spring when the ice thaws, *poof!* The sand falls in a uniform layer over the basin floor. Sand works like an inorganic mulch, shading out weeds and, like the finings in a beer crock, holding down sediment. In muddy ponds, it's a good carpet material for the basin floor. One of my neighbors was able to use a sand drop to eliminate the slimy bottom in her family's pond, along with snakes and leeches. True, the sand drop does fill in the pond to a minute degree, but it's not often done, and it sure beats herbicides.

The sand drop technique works well for depositing boulders in the pond. Stones falling into the center of the basin can provide a shady retreat for fish. Or they can be arranged to create a diving rock, a foundation for a pier or platform, or an island, welcomed by waterfowl where dogs are a bother.

It seems natural to extend the drop technique to include lime, fertilizer, or precipitating agents, sometimes used by pond keepers as a tonic for ailing waters. Take care that these ingredients are not flushed out of the pond with spring runoff: Concentrate the drop upstream, away from the spillway area.

Icing can mean trouble, too. Late in autumn when my

pond begins to freeze, I watch the frothy inflow harden into a starry glaze, like a miniature Milky Way. Those stars are bubbles of air caught in the ice, and they signal the start of a spell of lowered oxygen levels in the water, potentially fatal for fish.

The trout here need about five parts per million dissolved oxygen in winter; other fish that winter over under ice have similar requirements. All may be subject to oxygen starvation due to overcrowding, underwater vegetation decay, and lack of light to stimulate photosynthesis. So far I've never experienced any winterkills, and my stock has climbed to a winter peak of sixty eight-inch brook trout— not bad for an eighth-acre pond with no supplemental feed. Proper pond construction accounts for most of my successful defense against winter oxygen starvation. At least five feet of water under the ice is recommended in these north-country parts. Besides, the pond is too young for a massive vegetation die-off. But there's another reason that ice hasn't choked the trout: broom hockey. Keeping a patch of ice clear for skating opens up the bottom of the pond to the sunlight necessary for oxygen production in submerged plants.

The pond keeper can also turn to the wind for help with aeration. Given at least a two-mph breeze, a Pondmaster water circulator will stir a hole in the ice and aerate the water. The Pondmaster and another larger wind-powered water circulator, the Lake Aid, are touted as year-round aerators, though I wouldn't count on much of a breeze in summer when oxygen levels are lowest. For summer aeration, motor-driven aerators provide the best insurance against fish kills.

In *A New Booke of Good Husbandry*, Bishop Dubravius recalls his hardest trial by ice. It was the Lenten carp harvest. The bishop's men had come to him complaining that the harvest was impossible. They had chopped a hole in the ice and lowered nets into the pond, but not a carp had stirred. Round and round the pond the men stampeded, trying to drive the fish into the nets. No luck. So the bishop took down a wagonload of earth to the pond. Opposite the hole his men had opened, Dubravius cut again. Then he wheeled over his wagon and dumped the earth into the water. An explosive burst of earth embroiled the pond in clouds of silt, and the frightened carp fled straight into the nets. Amen.

Spring

The main spring maintenance objective is to be a good midwife at the rebirth of the pond after its long dark winter. The pond wants to take in big gulps of fresh, richly aerated water and flush out last year's crud. You help. But beware: simultaneously the pond must be shielded against two threats that arrive with spring waters—erosion and silt.

The erosive, silting power of spring flood water is formidable. A stream that doubles its speed quadruples its load-carrying capacity. The more silt it carries, the greater its ability to erode. A vicious hydrologic cycle.

Moreover, at the same time that thawing snow and falling rain are adding to spring floodwaters, the shoreland heaves as frost works its way out of the ground. Spillways, ditches, and berms are undermined. Piping cracks and trash racks clog. In a few weeks of spring the pond is likely to suffer more damage than all the rest of the year.

As usual, good siting and construction make the best defense against reservoir wear and tear. In spring the wise pond keeper will congratulate himself for steering clear of big stream inflows; even a small intermittent vein can deliver an avalanche of silt.

Throughout spring, water channels leading into and out

Riprapping the inflow.

of the pond should be cleaned and reinforced. Debris in the vein feeding the pond will decay, eating up oxygen and tipping up water temperatures; debris in the spillway will back up overflowing water, causing erosion around the spillway approach channel and shore, not to mention the chance for flooding. Spring is also time to check for ice damage to piping.

Mind the watershed above the pond, especially cultivated farmland or terrain doused with manure, chemicals, or garbage. Open upstream land will feed detritus into ponds. Diversion ditches and berms around the upstream hemisphere of the pond help detour silt, but don't dig them in spring! Refrain, too, early in the year, from logging, roadwork, or construction in the near upstream watershed.

Pipes that feed stream water to bypass ponds often clog in spring. A "digger dam" in the stream just *above* the intake pool will usually sweep silt around the pipe, and in conjunction with a screen and/or trash rack, will keep the inflow clear. (See Digger Pond chapter.) For clearest passage through rough spring waters, some pond keepers find it simplest to close off side pipes at the source.

In the book *Aquaculture,* authors Bardach, Ryther, and McClarney recommend keeping silt out of fish ponds with a saran filter, a plastic mesh akin to today's grain sack material. For ponds fed by sidepipe, they recommend capping the outlet with a saran sock, kind of a pond condom. For ponds with a natural channel feed, they suggest trapping silt in a saran-bottomed box at shoreline water level. Not a bad notion, especially where fish—or fish keepers—are vexed by especially silty waters.

Yet here in a forest watershed of tightly knit soils, my pond needs no filter. Besides, from the foot of the inflow I like to dive into the water, not into a box. So in spring I use an old logger's trick for clearing roughed-up streams.

I lay a hay bale crossways in the channel to filter out silt. Later, when the water warms up, I shovel out a wheelbarrow or two of spring silt, fine fill for the puddles that settled in the dam after excavation. The marsh marigolds that I planted in the inflow channel help hold the earth in place, too.

Stones cleared from the embankment after excavation become a thrifty resource, piled by the spillway for springtime repairs. This riprap can be paved in the inflow channel and along patches of muddy shore. Incidentally, rock paving is recommended both as an antidote for banks that erode under wind-whipped waves and as a barrier against fish poachers and pond unpluggers like otters and mink.

To finish off the rites of spring on a modern note, I suggest you look at that sulphurous bruise that appears on ponds thawing downwind of industrial smokestacks. All winter, the ice has been catching polluted snow and rain. When it melts, six months of accumulated acid rubbish sinks into the pond. It's a bad time to stock fish. Better wait a few weeks and let the pond flush. Those hockey clearings won't help much unless snow is moved off the pond, or at least as far as the spillway, where it will flush out quickly. Lime or wood ashes are a long-standing remedy for acid pH. Anywhere from 10 to 100 pounds of agricultural lime may be needed. It's best to test the water and correct in small doses. What's really needed, of course, is a dose of intelligence in high places.

Summer

Three typical problems come up in summer ponds: overgrowth of aquatic vegetation and algae, low water, and dead fish.

The emergence of aquatic vegetation and algae is just about inevitable in an earth pond. In fact, a certain amount of vegetation is fine nourishment, feeding oxygen to fish and other critters, and helps keep down sediment. For many warmwater fish, a bloom of algae means a rich pond. A healthy growth of algae is said to fade a bright object from sight beginning about eighteen inches underwater. For trout farmers, the water should be clearer, say Chablis compared to Bordeaux.

Excess algae and weeds make an obvious mess of pond structure and water quality. Clouds of algae ground swimmers, tangle fishing lines, clog spillways and pipes, and lure animals you don't want. Massive vegetation will drive up water temperatures, stressing fish; eventually large masses of vegetation die off, exhausting the oxygen supply and contributing to fishkills.

Again, good construction is the best maintenance. A deep pond with steep banks discourages weeds and algae. It's important to keep up water levels to discourage weeds from getting a toehold on the banks and to keep up conservation tactics, especially ditching away runoff that could feed vegetation. Summer is the time to fix fences, too; keeping animals off the shoreland prevents trampling of the banks.

For conservation agents, summer brings a deluge of phone calls from pond owners maddened by weeds and algae. Often, callers are left with the impression that the only solution is a bottle of chemicals or a dredging machine. Copper sulphate, Cutrine-Plus and Aquazine are just a few of the algicides and herbicides that I have seen recommended by conservation agencies and aquaculture literature. Dyes that shade out the sun and kill vegetation are also popular. (Dragline dredging makes an effective nonchemical cleanup but may cost as much as a new pond.)

There are several reasons why I would hesitate to douse a pond with chemicals. Who really knows the long-term effects of these solutions? Many algicides and herbicides have been on the market a short time, and there is little to gain in making your pond a guinea pig for the chemical industry. I can't imagine dumping herbicides in my pond without tainting the food chain all the way from the May fly larvae in the mud to the drinking water in my neighbors' springs and wells downstream. In fact, most herbicides and pesticides are used by commercial fish growers who know that there are natural, albeit slower, cleanup techniques, but complain that in the rush for profits there's no time for anything but the quick chemical fix. Alas, these growers are just discovering that their chemicals are backfiring, causing off-flavors in pond fish. And there's no profit in that, no matter how quickly fish grow. So, lately, there's been talk about "dewatering." That's the modern aquacultural lingo for Dubravius's favorite natural antiseptic: the drawdown.

By lowering the water level from a foot to completely empty the pond, the pond keeper can kill off aquatic vegetation and parasites, and restore water clarity and oxygen levels. A siphon hose or a pump is the simplest means for a drawdown. In ponds with bottom drains, it may be difficult to manage anything less than complete draining, and that's not always necessary, especially if the problem is simply a patch of shoreline weeds. A full drawdown is out of the question for a pond carrying fish or irrigating a garden—unless the pond keeper has another pond and can drawdown alternately.

During a drawdown the pond basin is exposed to the air and the sun, killing off algae and aquatic vegetation. Exposure to the elements also hastens decomposition of vegetation on the basin floor, leading to richer oxygen levels when the pond refills. A partial drawdown may occur naturally during hot and dry weather. The pond water level drops a foot or two without the pond keeper's lifting a finger.

This is the time to step in with a shovel or sickle to clean up the banks. It's a good idea to cut or pull weeds before seeds form, but be sure your weeding doesn't coincide with fish spawning, when eggs may be incubating in the reeds.

The complete drawdown—fully drained and fallowed for the summer—causes an antiseptic effect throughout the basin and enables the pond keeper to change the fish population and to get at the rich muck. Dredgings make a good

During drawdown . . .

topsoil spread or garden amendment, as long as they are composted first. A friend of mine beefed up his sandy front yard with fresh pond scrapings and wound up with a lawn full of cattails. On a garden, fresh dredgings can burn plants.

In 1600, in England, John Taverner published a treatise on the art of pond culture and orcharding, *Certaine Experiments Concerning Fish and Fruits*. It is recognized as one of the

. . . and after.

first studies of husbandry in the West based on observation and experiment rather than hearsay. Taverner recommended the drawdown as the ultimate pond cleanser. He summed up the effects of the drawdown:

> You shall avoid superfluous numbers of fish, which greatly hinder the growth and goodness of your greater fish. Secondly, by that means you shall so proportion your pond, that it shall never be overstored. Thirdly, by that means your water shall always be excellent sweet by reason it overfloweth such ground as hath taken the sun and ayre all sommer before.

Here in Orange County, I've watched several ponds clear up after summer-long drawdowns. The most dramatic was a small farm pond that had been neglected for years: clumps of algae clouded the surface, cattle trampled the banks, and pasture runoff leached into the water. After fencing his cattle downstream from the watershed, the pond keeper siphoned out the water with three garden hoses and left the basin exposed to the sun for the summer. A year later, refilled and stocked with trout, the pond sparkled.

Fish, too, may be enlisted for pond maintenance. For instance, carp are used to keep the canals of Holland clean. Down in Arkansas, Jim Malone is renowned for the diploid (reproducing) and triploid (non-reproducing) grass carp he raises to sell to pond keepers and waterway officials seeking nontoxic weed killers. One of his fish will down up to ten pounds of algae, moss, and weeds in a year. Yet many pond keepers must do without the help of this thrifty pond sweep. Game fishermen have lobbied to outlaw different varieties of twenty-four carp in all but twenty-three states: Alaska, Arkansas, Alabama, Connecticut, Delaware, Florida, Georgia, Hawaii, Idaho, Iowa, Illinois, Kansas, Kentucky, Mississippi, Nebraska, Nevada, New Mexico, New York, North Carolina, Ohio, South Carolina, Virginia, and Wyoming. Fishermen argue that the carp muddies streams and displaces game fish. Besides, with all those bones it's just *too* hard to clean! Elsewhere, especially in Asia, the carp is a popular food with reputed medicinal powers. Korean women relish the fish for prenatal health.

When I discovered that carp are verboten in Vermont I felt cheated. Must the pond keeper who can't take time out for a drawdown turn to chemicals?

Not at all, Jim Malone told me. "Don't take offense," he said, "but you should think of your trout as coldwater carp."

Malone is right. Trout have a reputation as fussy feeders, picky as spoiled Siamese cats; yet for three years I've watched my brook trout gain weight without an ounce of supplemental feed. I see them feast on the bottom as much as in the air: the water is as transparent as an aquarium. I recalled my neighbor's drawdown and follow-up trout stocking: clearly, the fish were pitching in to keep it clean. And I recalled an old Vermont tradition: to keep the farmhouse water clean, a trout was dropped in the well.

Turbid water is another problem in summer ponds. It's not unusual for a pond to cloud up after heavy rain, new ponds especially. In certain soils, for instance in Oklahoma, soil particles resist settling because of an unusual electrical charge that keeps them ricocheting around. Ponds in these soils tend toward permanent turbidity. The effect can be damaging: turbid water reduces light penetration and photosynthesis, smothers bottom life, cuts waste assimilation, and impairs spawning. Some pond keepers recommend agricultural lime or gypsum to clear turbid waters, with dosages ranging from ten to one hundred pounds per surface acre. But before I'd go shopping for agricultural chemicals, I'd try hay. Pond keepers have found that strewing old hay around the shallows helps clear turbid water, roughly seven to ten bales per surface acre. Decaying organic matter apparently reduces Brownian movement in the soil, causing particles to clump and settle.

The half-empty pond is a traditional sign of pond failure. Usually it's due to structural leakage or improper siting in dry terrain. Not that it's unusual for an earth pond to seep somewhat—only synthetic sealers or liners can make a pond truly watertight. What the pond keeper wants to prevent is *excessive* seepage. What's excessive? I knew one young lady whose new pond was a flop. At best in summer it held a couple of feet of muddy broth. Still, she was happy. "Honey, all I need is a place to roll around in the mud and I'm fine." Of course, commercial fish farmers can't afford that low-tide effect, and I wouldn't welcome it either.

Besides, new ponds, embankment ponds especially, tend to get off to leaky starts. During the first summer or two, a new pond may never reach its designed water level. Freshly excavated ponds are like coffee filters. At first the liquid streams right through; then gradually settling sediment and the weight of the water tightens the seal, with some help from the settling shoreland and new vegetation. Of course, some ponds plainly fail. How can you tell? The neighbors' ponds are full.

Fixing low-tide ponds begins with a search for leakage. Ponds with piping often leak around the outside of the pipe or through seams, gaskets, and valves. In most cases, unless a fitting can be easily replaced, pipe repair involves digging up the line to repair joints or to implant anti-seep collars.

In embankment ponds, the seal between the ground base and the bottom of the dam is another spot to watch. Hence the traditional emphasis on thorough clearing and preparation of the dam foundation ground, a wide base, and maybe a clay-filled center-line core trench. An extra half-hour of bulldozer compaction on the dam after construction also helps.

To Sherm Stebbins, the Randolph, Vermont, pond maker, the most maddening cause of dam leakage is improper siting. He told me about a job during his early days as a pond maker.

"My clients were dead set on a site on top of a ledge," Sherm said. Too rocky, he advised. They wouldn't hear of it, so Sherm built the pond. Driving by one afternoon, Sherm saw a dark stain spreading across the embankment. He raced up to the house to warn the owners that their dam was crumbling. That night they drained the pond, and Sherm brought back his bulldozer to tear apart the embankment. He packed in a layer of clay over the rocky base and rebuilt the dam. The pond filled. Again it leaked. So they drained it, and Sherm once more tore apart the dam, added more clay and let it fill. This time the dam held. Sherm warned me, "Never, never put in a pond where you don't trust the earth!"

Porous soil in the pond basin is another cause of leakage. A technique for sealing porous soil is to drain the pond and layer the basin with clay or bentonite, packed in with a sheepsfoot roller or dozer. Some pond keepers seal leaky basins with a plastic liner. The pond must be drained and lined with sand to cushion the plastic against puncture. Often, 20 mil plastic is spread over the basin, glued or heat welded at the edges, and then covered with another few inches of sand.

Sometimes the best solution for low-level ponds is more water. I watched one low pond fill up with a supplement of water from a specially dug well. Another was revived when the owner tapped an upstream brook with one hundred yards of four-inch PVC pipe. To aerate the water, he staked the pipe so that it tipped up at the outlet, splashing inflow on a rock set at the shoreline. (Usually it's well water that needs aeration; fish farmers are careful to check well water oxygen levels, splashing it over baffles or stones, if necessary.)

As always, the foremost cure for leaky ponds is to forestall it in the first place with proper siting. Use test pits and soil tests to check for clay. As Dubravius warned, "He that soweth in dust shall reap dust."

This past summer, late in August, four brook trout turned up dead in my pond. It wasn't a big fishkill, but it was a big disappointment. Those trout were the last of my biggest stocking—sixty fry put in two years before. It was 80°F throughout the pond that weekend, hotter by ten degrees than the pond had ever been. The experts say that brook trout begin to die at 77°F.

Later, I talked to an angler with thirty years of fishing Lake Champlain under his belt. He told me that it had been the hottest summer he'd experienced in Vermont. Worse, for the first time in memory, the walleyes wouldn't bite. Surface water had reached the high sixties, and the walleyes were lying low to avoid the heat. My friend is a snob about walleyes; he won't chase anything else; I'm crazy about brook trout. We lamented that if Vermont summers stayed so hot, our fishing habits would have to change.

I considered aerating the water and building a pier to cast extra shade, maybe even dumping in a load of ice cakes from an icehouse on the dam. But that seemed excessive against a more natural solution: rainbows. Rainbow trout are hardier than brookies; they can survive more stress, less oxygen, and temperatures up to 86°F. And if they don't taste like brookies, the difference is hardly worth the cost of a crop failure or mechanical surgery. Next summer, along with a gambler's crop of brookies, I'll be stocking rainbows.

Fall

Fall is busy on land, but on water, life quiets down. In fact, there's little to do, unless you count catching trout. When trout reach ten to twelve inches it's time to make room for next year's crop. Otherwise you might see your big fish eat your stock. I never catch all the trout at once. Instead, the pond is a live cooler from September through November, and I harvest when the pan is hot. No fancy tackle involved, only an old spinning reel, a sharp hook with the barb filed off, worms or grasshoppers or bacon, and a bucket.

Laying down the pond for winter does mean keeping out leaves. Decaying leaves eat up oxygen under the ice and then come back to haunt you as slimy algae in summer. Here it's easy to rake submerged leaves from shore. In cool weather the water clears up, and sunken debris is in clear sight. There's not much: this is a self-cleaning pond. High up on a windy slope, the pond is swept by westerlies that shepherd leaves to the east bank where the spillway current draws them off. Only the leaves from some birches, maples, and one old apple tree are trapped against the spillway fish fence. It's simple to rake them away. On a breezy site the pond with downwind spillway grooms itself.

A final seasonal ritual comes with the first skating ice. My shadow glides beneath the transparent ice, skates carving powdery white calligraphy on the frozen pond. A brush pile stands on the dam, collected throughout the summer and fall. Twilight falls. I fire the brush. A deep orange reflection lights on the ice: the pond keeper's harvest moon.

Troubleshooting Guide

Symptoms	Problem	Solution	Page Reference
Algae	Inadequate exchange of fresh water	Increase inflow	109–110, 113–115
	Pond too shallow and/or warm	Dredge deeper; increase inflow	113–115, 130
	Excessive nutrients flowing into pond	Eliminate nutrient inflow; use biological methods to decompose or eliminate nutrients; use aeration	102–110, 126–136
Aquatic weeds, emergent	Taking over pond edges, basin	Use biological methods; manually remove weeds; dredge; draw down	113–115, 126–136
Aquatic weed, submerged	Taking over pond	Use biological methods; manually remove weeds; dredge; draw down	113–115, 126–136
Embankment erosion	Slope too steep; poor soils	Reseed and mulch; sod; rip rap; add fill to flatten slope	71, 85, 123, 125, 86–89
Low water level	Leaks in porous soil, ledge, or piping	Seal basin with clay or artificial liner; repair or eliminate piping	71, 84–86, 122–125, 115–122
Low water level	Inadequate inflow; embankment and/or spillway too high	Increase inflow; improve natural runoff; adjust spillway and/or embankment level	109–110, 113–121
Overtopping; flooding	Frozen outlet pipe; spillway blocked by ice	Thaw pipe; reopen spillway; repair outlet	115–121
Overtopping; flooding	Watershed drainage too large for spillway capacity	Enlarge outlet pipe; enlarge spillway; divert inflow; install emergency spillway	61, 113–121

Overtopping	Outlet pipe or spillway blocked by debris or beavers	Clean pipe or spillway; add trash guard to outlet; trap beavers; install anti-beaver flumes; consult game department officer for assistance	61, 113–125
Low water level	Holes in basin or embankment caused by muskrats	Trap muskrats	124
Low water level	New pond	Allow pond to seal naturally	71, 109, 113
Siltation; sediment	Erosion of inflow stream; erosion of watershed	Prevent erosion of inflow stream/watershed	113–115
Stagnant water	Inadequate exchange of fresh water; basin too shallow	Increase inflow; dredge basin; aeration	113–115, 130–136
Turbid Water	Clay has not settled	Use hay or gypsum to precipitate clay	108
Fishkill	Inadequate dissolved oxygen	Increase inflow; aeration; reduce fish population; eliminate dead vegetation	127, *see Appendix for test kits*
Fishkill	Overheated water	Add cooler water; create shade; deepen pond	*see Appendix for aquatic services*
Fishkill	Toxic chemicals	Test water	
Fishkill	Disease	Consult fisheries biologist	
Fish disappear	Herons; king fishers	Use scare-away devices; netting; do not shoot: protected species	39–41, *see Appendix for scare away devices*
Fish disappear	Leaving via spillway	Screen outlet stream	29

Pond Repairs

All ponds are divided into three parts: the inflow, the basin, and the outflow. The inflow may be a spring, stream, pipe, watershed runoff, groundwater, or a combination. The basin consists of the pond bowl, adjacent shoreland, and, in the case of an embankment pond, the dam. The outflow may be a natural spillway, a piping system, sluice gate, or a combination of these. In some cases a dug pond will not have a visible inflow or outlet, but unless it's stagnant, ground water is flowing through. "Sky ponds" and other reservoirs that depend solely on precipitation have no ground water inflow.

Inflow brings the water, the basin holds it, and the outflow releases it. When a pond is in good shape, the three elements work together. Elementary stuff to be sure, until something goes wrong.

Inflows

Most ponds depend on a combination of several water sources. When operating properly, a pond will have good water volume and adequate exchange, or overflow, to ensure against stagnation. When the inflow goes awry, a pond will have either too much water or too little, and perhaps siltation due to erosion. The most common problem with inflow is lack of sufficient water to sustain pond level and ensure a healthy exchange. The problem might be simply drought. Or perhaps the pond was built with the option of eventually developing a supplementary water source, if needed. Or it's simply sited incorrectly.

New ponds often take a year or two to seal naturally, so it may be premature to look for extra water or search for leaks until the pond has a chance to settle. Moreover, it may be difficult to decide if low water is due to inadequate inflow or a leak. Since it's usually easier to add water than repair a leaky basin, solutions for low water usually begin with an examination of supplementary water potential. Even if the pond does leak, a fresh source of water may compensate for the loss.

Before developing new water sources, it's important to determine if existing inflows are clogged or cut off. Spring flows and small streams often become overgrown with vegetation or clogged with silt. A previously reliable source of water may back up and soak the ground above the pond before reaching the basin. I worked on one pond where a pipe carrying spring flow to the shoreline had been crushed and sealed shut by an excavator during a cleanup job. It was just enough of a loss to slow down the exchange to a point where algae bloomed and covered the pond. A cleanout won't be especially helpful for a pond that's short of water.

Because of the potential for erosion, cleaning out feeder streams or bringing in supplementary inflows directly may bring in silt. It's important to do stream work during dry weather and to stabilize the channel upon completion. If a stream is prone to erosion, it often makes better sense to contain the water in a pipe. Piping prevents erosion and enables the owner to control the flow, which can be helpful during repairs. Adding a cutoff valve, along with an alternative channel for the water so that inflow can be diverted around the pond, makes it possible to keep the pond dry during maintenance work. Piping also prevents water loss due to seepage. If animals are pastured on inflow areas it may be necessary to pipe water in to prevent damage from trampling.

Piping a stream into a pond can be tricky. It's necessary to create a pool that will feed the bypass pipe and yet not readily fill with silt. Often a dam is constructed upstream of the pool so that water cascading over the top actually carves out the pool below, keeping it relatively silt-free (see Digger Pond). Usually the pipe is covered with stone or encased in a perforated concrete or steel box to filter out debris and silt.

Flexible plastic pipe is often used to bring in extra water and can be buried or left above ground, depending on winter use. Normally an above-ground pipe should be drained in winter if there is any chance of freezing. A pipe buried below frost line will run in cold weather, as long as the pickup source doesn't dry up or freeze. If the pond is used in winter, for fish culture or skating, for instance, the water line will have to be frost-proofed or the water level may drop due to icing in the pipe. It's important to bury the pipe with as few dips and rises as possible to ensure against air locks or silt clogging the line. A vent in the pipe sometimes helps prevent air locks. A pipe that flows downhill with no obstructions will be easy to drain, which is helpful in winter. Burying the line also keeps the water cooler in summer, which may or may not be helpful depending on the temperature you or your fish like to swim in.

Flexible corrugated construction pipe, sometimes called "elephant trunk," is becoming popular in pond systems. Four-inch elephant trunk delivers a large volume of water and is easily maneuvered. Elephant trunk can be used in temporary setups quite effectively to bring cold stream or well water to a trout pond in summer, and during pond construction to prevent water flowing into the pond from

eroding the exposed soil. I've also seen it used as a pond siphon hose that doubled as a suction pipe to remove silt.

If piping seems unnecessary or too expensive, channeling supplementary water directly into the pond may be the most practical. Dry weather is best for digging, and upon completion it's important to stabilize the channel with rock riprap and/or vegetative reinforcement. Often a small silt basin is dug just upstream of the pond to catch silt before it reaches the pond. This pocket can be cleaned out as needed, by hand or machine, without disturbing the pond.

If no supplementary stream or well is available, pond owners sometimes cut drainage ditches in the watershed above the pond to channel in water. The ditches are usually filled with stone over perforated plastic pipe. As a last-ditch resort, an artesian well may be drilled for extra water, although hitting a rich vein is never certain. If leakage is suspected, balance the estimated cost of bringing in water against that of attempting to improve the pond's water-retaining ability.

Erosion of the feeder stream, and consequent siltation of the pond, is a common inflow problem. It's not unusual for ponds to require cleanouts near the inflow every five or ten years. Poorly designed ponds, particularly if excavated during wet weather, can fill up with silt during their first year where the soil is unstable. Thus it's best to wait for dry weather for digging, and perhaps divert channel inflows away from the pond or through the basin via pipe during construction. When work is complete, the water can be returned to the pond after inflow channels are stabilized with riprap or piping. Riprap is effective where silt slows down stream flow. Such incoming water channels should be cleaned out and lined with stone to facilitate the flow, reduce erosion, and discourage algae.

In addition to using piping and silt basins, inflows can

be stabilized by filtration. Hay bales are sometimes used in stream channels to retard the movement of silt. Establishing a vegetative strip may also help, whether it be native grasses or sod.

Rock riprap is one of the most common solutions to inflow erosion. It's important not to use large stones that leave wide gaps between them. In areas where the soil is especially silty and unstable it may be helpful to lay down a bed of gravel before applying the riprap.

Ponds can also suffer from an inflow of too much water. A good example is the story of Runaway Pond in Glover, Vermont. In 1810, the operator of a grist mill in Glover decided that he needed a more reliable source of power for his water wheel, so he had a ditch dug from his existing pond up to another reservoir at a higher elevation. The idea was to channel the new pond into the original, but when the channel was complete and the water rushed down, the stream inundated the mill pond. The pond overtopped, the embankment blew, the mill was destroyed, and so was half the town. Moral: don't add more water than your pond can handle. The miller's mistake was in not building a control gate on the higher pond so that he could regulate the inflow.

Excavated ponds that lie in wet lowlands may be damaged by flood waters. Fortunately most excavated ponds, even if flooded, pose little threat downstream. Damage from flooding may involve siltation or contamination from upstream pollution, and loss of fish. It's possible to build a protective berm upstream as a barrier against flooding. The berm's effectiveness will depend on the height of the berm and the level of flooding. Material excavated during construction can be used to build the berm. A more natural look can be achieved by using earth excavated from the pond to build up a complete surrounding shore area a foot or two higher than the existing terrain. Like an island, the pond-shore complex sits above ground level, well protected against flooding. Utilizing excavated material close to the pond, rather than trucking it away, may also save on construction costs.

Outlets

A well-designed outlet can mean years of trouble-free pond operation. Whether it's a natural earth spillway, a sluice gate, or a pipe, the outlet has to be sturdy enough to funnel pond overflow year round, and withstand the upheavals of winter frost and ice. Natural spillways are favored by pond designers who want to eliminate pipe costs and risks of leakage. The natural look of a pond overflow stream and its potential for landscaping also appeals to many pond owners. Excavated ponds often feature natural spillways because of the impracticality and expense of installing lengthy drain pipe in valley terrain. On the other hand, a pipe outlet may seem attractive to some pond owners who wish to create a seamless shore, prevent erosion, or have the ability to quickly drain the pond, vary the water level, or divert the overflow for irrigation, hydropower, or aquaculture.

The simplest pond outlet is a natural earth spillway. It may be prone to erosion, but usually this is overcome with stone, ledge, or other reinforcing material. Particularly in new ponds, earth spillways can erode dramatically if not adequately lined. Field or brook stone, or rock riprap, is generally used. Often a natural spillway will utilize a large rock or ledge at the crest of the spillway to prevent erosion. On-site ledge may be incorporated into a design to function as the spillway. I've seen spillways covered with a protective layer of concrete, but the concrete is often undermined by runoff and ice.

It's not unusual for a new pond to require an extra load

Leakage around this improperly installed overflow pipe led to spillway failure.

The overflow was repaired by removing the pipe and building a natural spillway lined with crushed stone.

of stone to reinforce a natural spillway after the pond overflows the first season. Ponds with especially steep overflows will be most susceptible to erosion. A spillway that descends in a curve will not wash out as readily as one with a straight drop. Sod can be used to help stabilize the spillway banks. Once vegetation is reestablished and the channel stabilizes, a natural spillway may need little attention. One pond owner commented to me that she liked a natural spillway because she could see what was happening. Because of leakage, she had replaced the original horizontal drain pipe with a natural spillway. She added flat stones in steps to create a waterfall effect.

It's important to make sure that leaves and other debris don't clog the channel, especially if wire mesh is used to keep in fish. Such fencing can plug up. Sometimes a spillway will draw floating leaves and debris to the outlet where it can be skimmed or raked out. This is especially true if the spillway is sited leeward of prevailing winds.

If a spillway does need repairs or additional stone, be sure not to raise the water level of the pond to a point where it might inadvertently flood the dam. In some cases a small amount of erosion might be tolerable in one pond but not another. I've seen farms where fencing that crossed the spillway became ineffective because of erosion. In a case like that it may be necessary to pipe out the overflow. Frequent traffic across a spillway might also destabilize the channel and require a pipe outlet.

Ponds are usually piped through either a horizontal or slightly tilted overflow, or through what's called a trickle tube (also known as a drop inlet). A horizontal pipe is relatively simple to install just a foot or so below shore level, with a slight downward tilt. The trickle tube is a vertical drain open at the water level and coupled by an elbow to an outlet pipe near the bottom of the pond basin. Pipes are

often used in embankment ponds because they offer no-erosion overflow as well as the option of attaching a drain for repairs, clean-outs, and fish harvests. Pond owners who need to drive across the spillway prefer piped spillways.

Unless carefully installed, overflow pipe is vulnerable to an assortment of maladies. Because they often lie above frost level, horizontal water level overflows are especially subject to ice damage in winter. If the ground freezes and shifts the pipe, it's easy for overflow to sneak underneath. During spring runoff as the overflow increases, the ground beneath the pipe erodes and can drain the pond, damaging the embankment in the process. Chances for this kind of

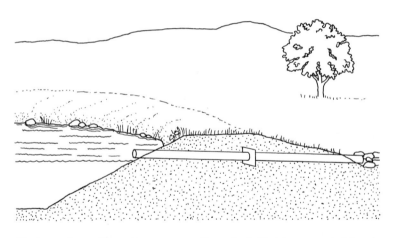

Horizontal overflow pipes are sometimes installed in excavated ponds where terrain prevents the use of drop-inlet systems. Because the pipe is often installed in shallow ground, it may be subject to frost heaving and subsequent leakage. Anti-seep collars should be used. Improvised anti-seep collars of asphalt can be painted on to impede leakage around the exterior of the pipe. To prevent creation of high freeboard, tandem pipes may be installed to carry off overflow.

blowout are greatly reduced if one or more anti-seep collars are fitted around the pipe prior to installation. Depending on whether plastic or steel pipe is used, the collars may be plastic, steel, or concrete. Tar is used to seal the seam. Plastic pipe is becoming popular with pond builders because of low cost and ease of handling and installation. It's light, no welding is required, and it won't rust. Because water moves with less resistance through smooth plastic pipe than through corrugated steel, smaller diameter pipes can be used. Some veteran pond builders are skeptical about the longevity of plastic pipe, and its susceptibility to ice damage. Thus double-riveted, asphalt-coated culvert pipe is often specified by state or federal engineers, especially for larger ponds. It's important that culvert pipe be carefully coupled together using asphalt caulking and then banded tight and welded.

A leak or modest amount of erosion around a horizontal pipe should not be difficult to fix. One resourceful pond owner told me about a shortcut remedy he devised for a water-level horizontal outlet that was leaking around the outside. He tamped down the earth above the pipe with a heavy log and the leak stopped.

However, tearing up a trickle tube and drain deeply embedded in a dam is another matter. Such repairs can be expensive and don't always work. Tearing apart the dam may lead to subsequent leakage unrelated to the pipe, because it's difficult to restore the integrity of the dam core. It's not unusual for pond owners with leaky or eroded piping to remove the pipe completely, refill the dam with earth, and then channel the overflow down a natural spillway. I once saw a leaky trickle tube filled with concrete to solve matters; an alternate natural spillway replaced it.

George Williams, a pond builder in Cavendish, Vermont, recalls an outlet that had to be dug up and repaired twice, and it continued to leak. He finally discovered small holes drilled into the pipe. The holes had been used for wires to help secure the pipe during transportation. He repaired the holes and the outlet worked.

Ice can do more than displace a horizontal outlet. When a trickle tube is installed so that the top several feet of pipe stand in open water, the pipe is vulnerable to damage from ice movement. I've heard of ice actually lifting a plastic trickle tube right out of the outlet elbow so that the pond emptied. Trickle tubes also can be pushed around by ice so they crack and leak. It makes sense to install the trickle tube close to shore so that only a foot or two isn't packed in earth.

Installing the pipe in solidly compacted, water-retaining soil is essential. One of the worst pond blowouts I've seen occurred in a pond that had been designed with "sand doughnuts" to serve as anti-seep collars. The drain pipe had been installed with several rings of sand around the pipe, intended to prevent seepage. Water found its way through the sand, and during spring runoff the dam tore open. By the time the pond emptied, a half-mile of town road had been destroyed. Repair fees and legal expenses exceeded the original construction costs.

In addition to making sure any pond overflow system near a public road is floodproof, it's important not to locate outlets too close to roadways. Water-saturated roadbeds are easily damaged by traffic and, because they're plowed in winter, may freeze and lead to icing in nearby pipe.

In cold climates, an outlet pipe exposed to the air for any great length at the downstream end may act like an ice tray, freezing and blocking overflow. The outlet should be cut off close to the earth it's installed in, making sure that the surrounding area is reinforced to prevent erosion.

Outlet pipes can become plugged with leaves and other

pond debris. Flat mesh screens and trash racks are sometimes used to keep pipes from plugging. It's important to make sure the mesh isn't so small that debris builds up and stops the outflow. If the pond owner occasionally cleans the outlet trash rack, or screen, the chances for plugging are reduced. Outlet cleaning is another good reason to site the pipe close to shore.

Outlet pipes can be plugged by animals. Beavers may block up outlet piping in an effort to raise the pond water level. It might not take long to clear the outlet at first, but beavers are persistent critters, and the pond owner may find himself in a daily struggle to prevent flooding. There are several ways to deal with beavers. They can be trapped or shot, depending on local laws and the sympathy level of the landowner. Dynamite is sometimes used to blow out beaver dams that jeopardize a pond or pose a threat downstream. Dynamite can also be used in the lodge to kill beavers and prevent another family from taking up residency.

But these are drastic measures, in many states against the law, and certainly not in tune with most pond owners I know. Thus, beaver inhibitors have been designed for pond outlets. The simplest is a mesh screen to prevent the animal from inserting brush or mud into the pipe. However, it's not unusual for a beaver to pack enough debris against the outlet screen to plug it, and more complicated solutions are required. One pond builder I know recommends building a dock over the outlet pipe and then wrapping the structure in wire mesh, right down to the bottom of the pilings, similar to a large trash rack. Vertical baffles on the outlet can also hinder beavers. Preventing beavers from damming a natural spillway may require more than physical removal of brush.

Rust is another problem that may occur with metal pip-ing. Leaks in piping usually lead to a drop in the water level, and replacement of the piping is necessary. Small leaks may not affect the water level, but it's not unusual for the area around the outlet pipe to become muddy because of this seepage. Depending on the severity of the problem, repairs may be necessary.

Some pond owners like to see a rather high water level, which may not be possible with a horizontal outlet pipe designed to carry substantial storm water. For instance a twelve-inch diameter pipe set under twelve inches of earth means that water will begin overflowing twenty-four inches below shore level. Some pond designers install two or three smaller pipes which together can accommodate the overflow but needn't be set so deep.

Outlet pipes and drains may be fitted with valves to control overflow. These can be quite costly and require expensive installation. Simple open/shut gates can be fitted to drains to cut costs. Bear in mind that for every plumbing feature added to a pond, also added is the potential for a leak.

Sluice gates offer some water level control, and in certain cases, a drain option. The sluiceway usually consists of wood or concrete abutments at the sides of the outflow channel, with a wood or steel gate that can be adjusted to raise or lower the water level. Sometimes planks are inserted or removed to change the water level. Relatively inexpensive wood sluiceways can be installed in small ponds, but design and construction costs for larger concrete structures may be high. Sluiceway damage usually involves erosion around the abutments or wing dikes, or under the foundation below the gate. Sluiceway repairs usually involve emptying the pond and rebuilding the abutments. Replacing the gate with a pipe outlet is often the most economical solution.

A small basin dug in the inflow stream just above this pond catches silt and prevents pond sedimentation. The basin can be cleaned out periodically without disturbing the pond.

The Basin

The heart of the pond structure is the basin. It has to absorb ground water, receive rainwater and surface level inflows, and hold both its shape and water. Keeping a healthy water level is the pond owner's greatest challenge. Of all the ills that afflict ponds—algae, aquatic weeds, siltation, eutrophication, and other maladies—leaks are the most common. Since none of us can see underground, leaks are the most difficult pond problem to identify and remedy, and they can develop from many different construction flaws or site conditions.

Keep in mind that all natural earth ponds leak—seep is a better word. Unless a pond is static, water is constantly flowing in and out of the basin. The idea is to keep the seepage to a minimum so that the desired water level and healthy exchange of fresh water can be maintained.

How do you know when a pond is leaking? It's not unusual for pond water levels to drop a foot, maybe more, naturally, during hot, dry weather. Some don't. It all depends on the local water conditions, pond soil and construction, and weather. New ponds sometimes take time to seal after construction so it may be premature to think about repair work before observing the pond through its first summer or two. Ponds sometimes will fill up after construction, during wet weather, and then drop as the precipitation falls off. Each pond has a distinct personality, and after several years of observation a pond owner can usually determine whether a pond water level drop is seasonal, weather-related, or more serious.

Significant leakage is usually due to excessively porous soil. Sandy soil, gravel, shale, and ledge in the basin can cause leakage. Good pond soil usually contains ten to twenty percent clay, sometimes more. It's not uncommon for a pond basin to include good clay soil and more porous material. Water leaks through the pervious soil, and that's where repairs should be made.

It's difficult if not impossible to repair a leak without draining the pond. However, determining the location of the leak may begin while the pond is holding water. Embankment ponds sometimes show evidence of leakage on the back side of the dam. Examining the outer bank may reveal especially wet areas or unusually tall grass or vegetation nourished by extra water. Another leak-locating technique is to dig a channel around the outside of the pond, at the base of the dam, with an additional ditch to keep the channel from filling with water. Examining the channel may reveal where water is leaking from the structure. Vegetable dyes are sometimes used in the pond water to help trace leakage. However, unless the dye reappears near the outside of the pond, the leak can't be pinpointed. Sometimes a "water witch" can dowse for leaks.

A little pond history helps leak detection. In the case of an embankment pond, find out if the dam was "keyed in." Good pond builders dig a core trench in the base of the dam and compact in a layer of impervious soil before building up the embankment. Like a tongue-and-groove joint in carpentry, this key creates a solid bond between the base and the dam. It's also important that the base of the dam be stripped of vegetation before the embankment is built. If these two items were omitted, you have a pretty good idea where the trouble lies.

Ledge or a streak of sand may allow water to leak from the pond basin—straight down. There's no tracing that kind of leak with a channel or dye. The pond must be emptied, and even then you may have to guess exactly where the leak originates. Depending on pond design and terrain, the basin should be emptied by drain pipe, pump, or siphon hose. When the basin is empty, it may be possible to detect ledge or gravel patches that might be leaking. A foot or two of clay applied over the suspected flaw, harrowed in or packed with a sheepsfoot roller, will often plug a leak. It's important not to dump the clay in a leaky pond, then refill it. The clay should be mixed with the basin soil and packed.

If good clay is available on site, it's the most economical solution. Otherwise clay is often trucked to the site. For those who live in areas where good clay is not readily available, bentonite is an alternative. Bentonite is a natural clay sealant that swells as much as twenty times its size when wet. It can be purchased in powder or granular form through aquacultural suppliers and well-drilling firms. Bentonite is generally applied "in the dry" at a rate of one

pound per square foot, mixed with the pond material with a light harrow, then packed down. Simply dumping it from a rowboat into a leaky pond is not likely to remedy the problem.

Plastic or rubber liners are often used to seal leaky ponds. Liners are manufactured in various thicknesses with optional ultraviolet light resistance to retard decay caused by sunlight. Liners are popular in small water garden pools, golf course hazards, and waste-water treatment lagoons. Because they cut off incoming ground water as well as leaks, liners are not usually used in ponds that depend on springs, unless only a portion of the pond is lined. When liners are used in spring-fed ponds, a drain may be required to prevent

This pond is being cleaned out and enlarged.

To prevent erosion, the inlet is lined with crushed stone.

displacement of the plastic. Liners should be installed on smooth terrain, preferably sand, to prevent tearing. Another layer of sand is often used above the liner as further protection.

Aquaculturists at the New Alchemy Institute in East Falmouth, Massachusetts, report success with experiments using a traditional sealing method borrowed from Russia. They create a "gley" by cutting grass and other green vegetation and packing it six to eight inches thick in the pond basin, then trampling it by foot. The gley sits for two weeks and rots, but it doesn't decompose because it becomes anaerobic. The gley forms a gel, and after two weeks the pond is filled. A gley lining will hold water for a couple of years or more.

Sometimes concrete or ferroconcrete (concrete with wire reinforcement) is used to patch pond leaks. I've heard of wooden pilings being driven into an embankment to create an underground wall against leaking. I've also heard suggestions that both diatomaceous earth and ashes can be used to seal pond soil, but seen no proof.

Since water loss can occur because of defective piping, it's important to check basin drain outlets for signs of leakage. Be sure that water is not finding its way out around the outside of the pipe, as well as through it. Be sure also that drain valves are shut tight.

Leaks can occur because of muskrats or other burrowing animals digging in the embankment. Muskrats sometimes burrow in a pond basin and their tunnels eventually leak water out of the pond. It may be necessary to trap the animals.

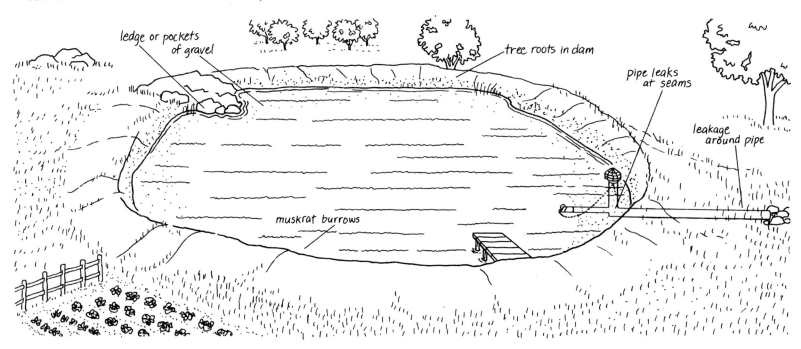

Tree roots incorporated in the dam or basin during construction may rot and open up leaks. It's important not to bury vegetation in the structure during construction. Tree roots growing in a pond dam can also cause leakage, which is why pond builders advise against planting trees on pond embankments.

Earth ponds, especially embankment ponds, are particularly vulnerable to internal and external erosion. Sloughing, or slumping as it's sometimes called, usually occurs inside a pond with overly steep slopes. The fill slides, and the pond loses its shape, perhaps leading to leakage or a weed problem.

Thus, while pond builders often disagree about things like spillway design, piping materials, or the best fish to stock, they usually agree about the slope angles inside and outside the pond. Inside, the slope should be no steeper than 2:1 in dug ponds (two feet horizontally for each foot vertically), and closer to 3:1 in embankment ponds. Slopes closer to 4:1 are used in ponds where livestock or swimmers get into the water. Outside slopes no steeper than 2:1 discourage erosion, and flatter slopes make mowing and maintenance easier. Slope angles also depend on the stability of the fill, and especially silty, erodible material requires flatter slopes.

It's important not to make the inside slopes too flat because they will foster weeds and algae. One solution for swimming areas is to carve out a beach and fill it with sand. The sand will serve as a mulch against weeds.

Ponds constructed on steep slopes may require shoring up in some areas. Where slopes are steeper than 2:1, stones are often used to build retaining walls to keep the basin from slumping. Besides adhering to these slope angles, careful pond builders often let fill material drain before building an embankment. By letting the water drain out of the material excavated for embankment construction, the fill is easier to work with and will not settle as much after construction. Also, pond builders often allow the finished basin to sit for several weeks before filling it with water. Warm sunlight on a newly constructed pond has the effect of baking the structure and sealing it, much like pottery in a ceramic oven.

Controlling Pond Weeds and Algae

Not long ago I attended a pond ecology seminar in northern New England. A group of forty or so pond owners gathered beside a side-hill swimming hole to soak up some wisdom about limnology, the study of freshwater lakes and ponds. The seminar was conducted by a conservation biologist, and after a lengthy discussion of pond use, water testing, fish stocking, and other aspects of pond management, she called for questions.

"What do I do about these pond weeds?" one fellow asked, holding up a bouquet of sedges. Another man complained that his pond was filled with clumps of algae. More hands shot up. "How do I get rid of cattails?" a woman asked. Quickly it became clear that almost everyone there had a problem with weeds, algae, or both.

The biologist suggested manual removal of weeds—pulling sedges, cutting cattails off below water level, and raking up algae. But many in the audience complained that they had tried manual removal, failed, and given up. The talk turned to chemical algicides and herbicides—copper sulphate, Cutrine, Rodeo. A comprehensive illustrated guide to pond vegetation was passed around. The book was published by a chemical company. I left. As I was walking back to my car a friend caught up with me, and I asked what he thought. "I hate to think of all these people going home to nuke their ponds," he said.

The problem seems to be that the traditional old farm pond is having an identity crisis. It's understandable that pond owners resist eutrophication, the natural aging process of a pond. However, in addition to functioning as a livestock drinking pool, fire pond, and irrigation supply, country ponds are now expected to have swimming pool water quality. Pond owners turn to chemicals the same way they might use chlorine in a pool. They overlook the fact that a pond is an ecological system connected to the natural world around it. Chemicals used to kill algae can also kill wildlife, and perhaps poison downstream water supplies.

Pond owners who use chemicals to eliminate pond plants and algae fall into the same trap apple growers got into with Alar. In the process of "saving" the crop, they ruin it.

Consider the effects of chemicals on a pond. Many algicides are fatal to fish. Chemical manufacturers warn that livestock and pets shouldn't drink from a treated pond for some time after application. How long is the water unsafe? When do you allow your kids to swim in it? Will your neighbor's well be affected by pond overflow? These are questions that no one can answer honestly. Ironically, while chemical algicides may seem effective at first, the conditions that led to infestation often remain, and the problem will recur, leading to yet another dose of poison.

Fortunately, there are many nontoxic alternatives to chemical weed and algae control. Manual removal of aquatic vegetation and algae can be effective. For example, spring is a good time to pull cattails, before the roots are deeply established. Later in the summer it's nearly impossible to uproot cattails. Cutting them below water level also prevents further spreading by seed. Sedges and other pond emergents can also be pulled.

The first algae blooms of the season usually occur during spring turnover, when the pond water "flips." Cold deep water rises to the surface, bringing with it nutrients that had settled to the bottom the previous year. This "nutrient soup" feeds the algae. Blooms of algae should be raked out of the water. Several manufacturers have designed algae and weed rakes and cutters for pond maintenance. It's important to remove algae and weeds from the pond so that decaying organic matter won't run back into the water, fortifying the nutrient soup.

Of course, if the purpose of the pond is to nurture wildlife, removing emergent plants from the pond edge deprives animals of their cover, exposing them to predators. Pond owners who like to encourage waterfowl to nest or lay over during migration usually allow a section of the shore to remain wild. The challenge is to keep the cattails and other vegetation in this zone from dominating the rest of the pond.

A well-designed pond will help discourage algae and weeds. Steep edges and deep water prevent weeds from getting a foothold. It's important to minimize shallow areas where the water heats up easily, encouraging algae. Bays and coves may look attractive, but wherever the water lies stagnant, algae finds a home. The fewer trees near shore, the less leaves shed on the pond, and that prevents the accumulation of "nutrient soup." A generous exchange of fresh water through the pond keeps oxygen levels up, which in turn contributes to a healthy food chain. Thus there's plenty of bacteria and pond life to feast on decaying organic matter.

Pond edges that can be mowed or hand cut discourage the spread of weeds. Erosion along the shore or inflow channels should be prevented. New ponds often benefit from a mulch of hay along the shore, which stabilizes the soil while grass seed takes root. Because using fertilizer near a pond often leads to algae and weed growth, builders may find it difficult to establish grass. Sod is sometimes used to create an instant lawn. Sod holds the soil in place, particularly in steep, wet areas, which is even more important than its attractive appearance.

Monitoring water quality may help a pond owner diagnose the source of weed or algae problems. High temperatures are often associated with aquatic growth problems. Water cooling may require tapping into a new source of water, or perhaps deepening the pond basin. Trees can help shade a pond, but keep in mind that deciduous trees shed leaves; evergreens do shed needles but in less volume. It's important to strike the right balance regarding shoreline plants. A fish farmer I know ran into trouble one summer after doing construction work around his pond. He stripped the vegetation and topsoil around the pond, the microclimate by the water heated up, the pond temperature rose, and the trout died.

A pond that is either too acidic or alkaline will not support the kind of aquatic life required to keep a pond healthy. Test kits are available for checking pond water. In general, fish and other pond life like a pH level somewhere between 6.5 and 9. Acidic ponds with low pH (less than 6.0) will stress fish and may lead to disease and death. A pond that is too acidic can be remedied by adding agricultural limestone. Extremely acidic water (less than 5.7) should be treated with one ton of agricultural limestone per surface acre of water. Moderately acid water (5.8 to 6.5) requires one-half ton per surface acre. Late fall or early spring is best for application. Spreading the limestone with a hand shovel from shore or from a boat is generally effective. It can also be spread on the ice where it will eventually drop in, come spring.

The amount of dissolved oxygen in pond water will affect

aquatic life and vegetation—and vice versa. Oxygen gets into pond water through the photosynthesis of underwater plant life, direct infusion from wind and wave action, and the splashing of incoming streams. When oxygen levels drop, bacteria lose their ability to decompose organic matter. Fish and other pond critters become stressed or die, and thus another element in the healthy food chain is removed. Maintaining healthy oxygen levels in a pond means increasing the chance that nutrients that feed algae will be digested before causing trouble.

Dissolved oxygen levels range from nearly zero parts per million to ten ppm or more. Trout need five ppm or better, while catfish can tolerate slightly lower levels. A pond with oxygen levels below three or four ppm may not support the bacteria and aquatic life necessary to help keep algae in check. Oxygen levels can be raised by splashing in supplementary water, cooling water temperatures, or using mechanical aerators or diffusers (see next chapter). In heavily stocked fish ponds, dangerously low oxygen levels may indicate that the carrying capacity of the pond has been exceeded and the population should be reduced.

Depriving algae and weeds of the sunlight necessary for growth is another nontoxic pond management technique. Sand is sometimes used as an underwater mulch to suppress aquatic vegetation. It is particularly effective in shallow shoreland areas where weeds and algae become quickly established. Not only does the sand eliminate vegetation, it also creates a beach area. Sand can be spread by hand shovel from shore or from a boat. Some pond owners take advantage of winter ice that allows them to spread sand over the pond area; in spring the ice melts and the sand drops. "Sand drops" are doubly effective because early spring is the best time to squelch aquatic vegetation before it gets established. It's important to make sure the sand is pure, without road salt added to prevent freezing. At least four to six inches are necessary to create an effective mulch. The remedy is temporary because after a few years of additional silt accumulation, weeds and algae have a new medium for growth.

Black plastic sheeting may be used to suppress vegetation, much as in garden mulching. The plastic is applied in affected areas and weighted down with rocks. Because of the difficulty of installing plastic sheeting, usually only a portion of the pond is treated at one time.

Construction-grade plastic has drawbacks. Because it is not ultraviolet-resistant, the material is unstable, degrades, and breaks down. After a season or two, the pond may be full of plastic shreds. Moreover, gases formed by decaying material on the pond bottom lift the plastic and displace it.

Several aquacultural suppliers manufacture bottom barriers of UV-resistant woven fiberglass, plastic, and nylon. These are more durable, and some feature slits or small holes to allow rising gases to pass through. The problem with these porous materials is that certain weeds, milfoil for instance, will take root in the small openings. Finally, silt can settle on any kind of bottom barrier, providing a medium for new weed growth and algae.

Nontoxic vegetable dyes can be used to reduce sunlight and suppress aquatic growth. Unlike sand or plastic, this shading technique must be used on the entire pond. To be effective, it should be applied early in spring. Its longevity will depend on how much the pond overflows. If the pond water exchange is substantial, the dye may be quickly diluted and ineffective. Another disadvantage to shading dyes is that by reducing sunlight, the growth of all vegetation will be retarded, as well as the supply of oxygen created by plant photosynthesis. Such loss of plant life and oxygen may jeopardize fish and other pond life.

Bacteria cultured for water quality improvement can be introduced to a pond to help break down organic material, decrease ammonia and nitrite, and lower biochemical oxygen demand. Essentially a concentration of normally appearing nonpathogenic bacteria, these microorganisms help speed up the decomposition of waste matter on the pond bottom, such as decaying fish feed, fecal material, dead weeds, and algae. Thus the nutrients for further algae and weed growth are reduced.

Nontoxic bacterial metabolizers are applied in raceways, aquariums, and other aquacultural systems, and are considered especially effective in waterfowl ponds. The advantage of bioaugmentation in water purification is that ponds may be cleaned without draining, dredging, or chemical treatment, and at relatively low cost. However, like most natural processes, bacterial water purification is not an overnight cure. To work efficiently, the bacteria need warm water and several weeks' time. Many pond owners who use bioaugmentation dose the water on a monthly basis, as preventive maintenance.

Fish can also be used for nontoxic biological weed control. Israeli carp, suckers, and white amur or grass carp are vegetarian fish that thrive on aquatic plants. If correctly stocked and managed they can keep a pond free of algae and many weeds, including cattails. The grass carp appears to be the most popular algae eater in North America. Usually sterile genetic hybrids are favored so that the fish will not reproduce and compete with game fish. Nevertheless, in many states, despite its inability to reproduce, the hybrid grass carp is illegal.

Stocked at a rate of ten fish per surface acre, the grass carp has a reputation for excellent algae control and is used in farm and golf course ponds. Usually fish are sold at the yearling stage of eight inches and will live seven to ten years. A mature fish will weigh twenty to thirty pounds. Unlike Israeli carp, which muddy the water during feeding, the grass carp causes minimum turbidity. Breeders claim grass carp stocked in bass or trout ponds will not harm other fish. Suppliers usually require a letter of approval from a pond owner's state natural resources department before shipping fish.

A pair of geese or a few ducks will help police algae and weeds while contributing their fecal matter to the nutrient buildup. It's the kind of tradeoff that some pond owners are happy to accept, and others aren't. A couple of geese on a quarter-acre pond aren't likely to add dramatically to the accumulation of organic waste, and an experiment in waterfowl weed control might be worth it on a troubled pond. To keep ducks around, clip their wings occasionally, and provide a predator-proof shelter. Ironically it is thought that some weed and algae problems begin with the arrival of wild waterfowl on a pond, carrying seeds on their feathers and in their digestive tracts.

The muskrat is another creature known for its appetite for aquatic plants, particularly cattails. But in addition to cattails, muskrats eat fish and burrow into embankments, often opening up leaks. Most pond owners prefer the cattails. Crayfish are also stocked to help control algae, with the caveat that they may burrow into an embankment and cause leaks.

Taking the water out of a pond can be an effective vegetation control method. Drawdowns, partial or complete, have been a mainstay of pond maintenance for centuries, dating back to ancient fish culture in China and medieval Europe. Algae and aquatic weeds cannot live without water, and when the pond is dried out, much of the vegetation dies.

Partial drawdowns of two to four feet will usually kill shoreline vegetation and algae. It's important to remove the dead plants so that seeds and nutrients don't find their way back into the pond upon refilling. Many pond owners drop the water level a couple of feet for a week or two, then rake the banks, refill the basin, and enjoy using the pond again.

Partial drawdowns have the advantage of not killing fish or putting a pond out of commission for a complete season. But algae and weeds are more effectively eradicated after complete drainage during both warm and cold weather. In addition to scorching aquatic vegetation, exposure to the warm sun and air hastens decomposition of waste materials on the bottom of the pond, reducing the amount of nutrients available for aquatic growth. During winter, in areas where frost penetrates the soil four inches or more, the roots of many exposed aquatic plants die. For example, one of the most effective nonchemical treatments for milfoil is the winter drawdown. Experiments with algae-eating insects are also underway in several states.

Building in the capacity for a complete drawdown is one of the best arguments for installing a drain during pond construction. Otherwise, some kind of siphon or pump mechanism is required to keep the pond dry. Often, if the timing is right, a pond without a drain can be pumped dry, and the curative powers of exposure to the elements works as it slowly refills. In professional aquaculture setups where the drawdown is used, two or more ponds are required so crops can be rotated. In traditional aquaculture, before the advent of hydraulic dredges and chemical algicides, ponds were routinely drawn down after a year or two, following the crop harvest. Today drawdowns are still favored as inexpensive, nonchemical maintenance treatment.

After ten years or so it's not unusual for sediment ac-cumulation and aquatic vegetation to exceed the curative powers of drawdowns, weed pulling, friendly bacteria, or algae-eating fish. It's time for dredging, the ultimate remedy for a silt- and plant-infested pond. The choice of dredging machinery depends on the size and location of the pond. A backhoe might be able to clean out a small pond, but larger basins often require a tracked excavator, bulldozer, or dragline.

It's possible for some dredging work to be done without draining the pond, particularly around the edge, but the result is often unsatisfactory. Working "in the wet" makes it impossible for the equipment operator to see what's happening underwater, and when the muddy water clears, the outcome is usually a rough pond bottom strewn with stones. Much of the silt that is stirred up in the dredging process settles once again on the bottom, and the removal of vegetation is only partial. Moreover, dredging breaks the seal that helps keep in water, and it's difficult if not impossible to reestablish the seal when working underwater.

Thus, before dredging, it's important to get the water out of the pond. If the pond has a drain, the task may be as simple as pulling the plug or opening a valve. However, the cap on the end of a pond drain is often buried in silt or otherwise jammed. There are several strategies for opening a stubborn drain. The plug or cap should be pulled straight out, rather than sideways, which may require enough rope to reach clear across the pond. It may take several men to pull the plug, or a come-along or tractor. Sometimes the line breaks before the drain opens. Often it's possible to ram a long pipe into the drain pipe from the outside, and break out the plug. I've seen a shotgun used to blow open a stuck plastic cap. Shooting would probably not be effective on heavy metal plugs or gates, and the ricochet might damage the pipe or injure someone. Diving underwater to open the drain is not recommended because of the danger of being sucked into the drain.

Ponds with no provision for drainage are usually pumped dry prior to dredging. Depending on the time of year and weather, the pump might be needed occasionally after the initial draining. It's best to avoid working in excessively wet weather because of the damage heavy equipment can do to the shoreland. Often a pump is equipped with an extra gas tank and run during the night prior to the next day's work. Water from the pond should not be pumped directly into a stream. Often hay bales are staked to the ground where the stream of pumped water runs to filter out sediment. If the terrain is right, a small pond may be siphoned dry with one or more garden hoses or larger flexible piping. Be sure to make provisions for the removal of dredged material prior to excavating. Usually this is set aside to drain before being used for landscaping or fill. Allowing the material to dry out makes it easier to work with, and also helps with decomposition of nutrients that build up underwater. If the pond owner has no use for the sediment, the contractor should remove it.

Often two machines are used during excavation. A bulldozer scrapes sediment, and an excavator or backhoe scoops it out of the pond into a truck, or on shore. If piled on shore, the material should not be so close to the pond edge that it damages the shoreline, or runs back into the pond.

The cleanout is a logical time to deal with any repairs or modifications that might slow down eutrophication in the future. It's a good time to steepen the slopes if they were shallow and had nurtured vegetation. An eroding feeder stream should be repaired, and perhaps a pocket dug in the channel to collect silt before it reaches the pond. This is also the time to consider installing a drain or fire hydrant. Perhaps a sand beach could be built to enhance swimming conditions and simultaneously mulch weeds.

Once the cleanout is complete, it's important to reestablish the pond seal. A good contractor often goes to a lot of trouble during construction to create a natural seal in the pond, and this seal should be reestablished after dredging. If any areas of porous material have been exposed, they should be covered with clay or other water barrier.

Finally, during refilling, the inflow can erode the exposed basin. Portable piping is often set up to bring in the water, and then removed. Planking can also be put down to protect the basin from erosion, and dismantled as the water level rises.

Healthy Ponds Need Plenty of Fresh Air

You've seen this kind of pond along a country road in the summer: bilious green, muck covered, deathly still. There might be a stand of cattails at one end of the pond and an island of algae offshore. It reminds you of an earache you came down with after diving in a livestock watering hole when you were a kid.

Funny thing, drive by the same pond in the fall, after the weather's chilled and there's been a good dousing of rain, and you hardly recognize it. If it weren't so cold you'd be tempted to pull over for a picnic.

What happened? A little bit of Mother Nature's homemade aeration. Some wind, some rain, cooler weather, and up goes the oxygen content in the water. The pond is transformed from a stagnant algae breeder into a clear pool.

Now imagine you own that pond. You know there are times of the year when the water is bright and algae-free. But never when you want to enjoy it. How do you transfer that clarity to the hot season when the pond undergoes its Jekyll and Hyde transformation?

In the past, pond owners (farmers for the most part) didn't interfere much with the natural aging process of a pond. Eutrophication, the gradual silting and weeding process, was allowed to progress until the pond had to be rebuilt, relocated, or abandoned. But in the last decade or two, ponds have become popular with a broad spectrum of people, and so have new techniques for pond maintenance and rejuvenation.

Considering the cost of construction, it makes good economic sense to prolong the pond life span without resorting to major excavation work or toxic chemical algicides. Factor in the spectre of drought, the greenhouse effect, and pollution, and it's easy to understand the growing concern about keeping ponds healthy. One of the simplest ways is to use aeration.

Aeration is the process of adding dissolved oxygen to water. Healthy levels of dissolved oxygen allow a pond to reach a level of biological activity that helps fish thrive and assists in the breakdown of decaying vegetation. The less the amount of undecomposed nutrients, the less the fuel for algae blooms and aquatic weeds.

Much of the time natural aeration is sufficient. Wind, rain, the splash of an incoming stream, and photosynthesis all contribute oxygen to the water. But on occasion oxygen levels drop to a point that threatens fish and water quality. Trout need at least five parts per million of dissolved oxygen; warm water fish like catfish, bass, and carp can do with three ppm.

Oxygen levels can be monitored with test kits ranging in price from under fifty dollars for liquid sample tests to several hundred for electronic meters.

Dangerously low oxygen levels usually occur in the summer because warm water will hold less dissolved oxygen than cool water. Subtract from an already depleted oxygen level the natural summertime evaporation of water from feeder springs and streams and the pond itself, and you have the formula for fishkills, algae blooms, funky smells, and the buildup of stagnant vegetation. Winter oxygen levels also may drop enough to threaten fish, especially in the north in heavily stocked ponds where months of ice and snow cover shut off light and, consequently, oxygen-producing photosynthesis.

A waterfall is nature's most effective aerator. A cascading waterfall performs the two principal functions of a good aeration system: adding oxygen and circulating water. As a waterfall pours into a stream or river, it mixes bubbles of air into the water and simultaneously sets up a current that disperses the oxygenated water downstream.

Even the most primitive sort of fountain acts as an aerator. Water tumbling down a series of steps is naturally aerated. For centuries, municipal water supply systems have used fountain and waterfall aeration to help oxygenate and thus purify drinking water. Most indoor aquariums use some sort of mechanical aeration. Aeration systems are used to treat waste water and sewage. Fish farmers use aeration to boost oxygen levels in order to increase production capacity. During a stretch of hot weather pond owners can stop a fishkill by rigging up a simple pump to draw water from the pond and splash it back in. Surprised by the first signs of a fishkill, fish farmers sometimes start an outboard motor to aerate the water.

But firing up a suction pump or outboard motor is awkward and uneconomical. Highly efficient aerators capable of treating hundreds of gallons per minute have been designed for recreational ponds, fish farms, and municipal drinking water and sewage treatment basins.

Surface Aerators

Surface aerators operate much like a miniature waterfall. A propeller close to water level splashes water into the air, and as it falls back into the pond, the water is oxygenated. Some surface splashers float on the water, some are installed on rigid posts in the water. Surface aerators are effective at building up a high level of dissolved oxygen quickly. Anglers fishing in ponds oxygenated by splash aerators often comment that the best place to find fish is close to the aerator, much like fish congregating in pools below waterfalls.

Surface aerators are popular in golf course ponds and other public waters because of their dramatic fountain effect, in addition to water-quality enhancement. Some aerator manufacturers offer splash aerators featuring flamboyant fountain sprays and multi-colored illumination. Night illumination adds more than just pretty lights. It creates an element of security.

Because of their capacity for quickly building up oxygen levels, splash aerators are popular with fish farmers maintaining intensively cultivated ponds. Lila Stutz-Lumbra manages the Waterland Trout Hatchery in Montgomery, Vermont, and uses several aerators. She prefers installing the aerators on floats.

"They're easier to move when we're netting fish or changing the aerator to another location," she said. "We keep track of the oxygen, and when it drops below safe level the aerator goes on. Eighty percent saturated is good. Last summer we had a pond with four parts per million one day. We turned on the aerator and the level was up to eight the next day." Stutz recommended that trout growers aerate during the summer on cloudy days and at night. "Running surface aerators on hot sunny days will raise the water temperature," she said. "Running them at night will help bring down the temperature."

Splash aerators do have their drawbacks. Because of the need for an electrical hookup in the water, special care must be taken to fuse the line to prevent accidental short circuits. For people who want to enjoy swimming as well as raising fish, it would be prudent to disconnect the splasher when bathing. The chance of lightning striking an electrical aerator also worries some pond owners.

Floating aerators require anchoring, usually a pair of mooring lines secured on shore. When one line is released, the aerator can be pulled in. Pond owners who swim and use boats must navigate around mooring lines or pull in the aerator. Splash aerators installed on rigid posts near shore enable pond owners to get around the problem of floating obstructions.

Most splash aerators are designed for winter use, and can be effective at keeping the ice open for waterfowl and maintaining oxygen levels for fish. Care must be taken during especially cold weather that ice doesn't form on the mechanism and sink or disable the unit.

The cost of operating a surface aerator depends on the oxygen requirements, the size of the pond, and the power of the unit. In general, aquaculturists figure that one horsepower is required for every surface acre. In heavily stocked ponds, the power might have to be increased. Splash aerators range in size from ⅙-horsepower to five horsepower and more. Prices range from under $400 and up. Operating

Problems with algae and low oxygen levels often can be remedied by using aerators like this mechanical splasher or underwater diffusion aerators (see photo on p. 98).

costs depend on the size of the unit and local electrical costs. For example, a ⅓-horsepower Fresh Flo aerator uses .42 kilowatts per hour. Thus, if your electrical cost is 7 cents per kw hour, aerator costs will run about 3 cents per hour or 72 cents per day.

Total costs will depend on frequency of use. A recreational pond owner may need to use aeration for a few weeks during the height of summer, perhaps only in the evening. A professional fish grower may require continuous aeration.

Diffusion Aerators

Diffusion aerators oxygenate the water from below the surface. A compressor on shore pumps air through flexible tubing to an underwater diffuser on the pond bottom. Air bubbles float up to the surface and thus oxygenate the water. To be effective, a diffuser should be set up at a depth of at least four to five feet to ensure adequate "hang time" as the bubbles rise and give off oxygen. Diffusers use less power than surface splashers. The ¼-horsepower Grovhac GenAIRator diffusion aerator uses .30 kw per hour.

A diffusion system not only adds valuable oxygen to the water, but creates a current that helps circulate the oxygenated water throughout a pond. One of the unique advantages of a diffuser is the ability to satisfy oxygen demand at the bottom of decaying vegetable matter, fish wastes, and other organic residue. Often because of temperature stratification which lowers the oxygen level at the bottom of the pond, the residue in this area does not readily decompose. As this layer of silt deepens it becomes an increasing source of gases toxic to fish, as well as nutrients for algae. A diffusion system takes oxygen down deep to increase the decomposition rate and thus slow sedimentation. It also creates an upward mixing current that vents toxic gases. Pond owners especially like diffusers because there is no

electrical hookup to run through the water, and no mooring lines to tangle up boats and swimmers.

Don and Peg Mohar live on the shore of a twenty-acre lake in Chesterton, Indiana. For the past several years the lake has been covered with algae during the summer. Nutrient-rich runoff from nearby farms contributed a deep layer of silt. The lake was a mess.

Together with eight other families living on the lake shore, the Mohars checked into different clean-up strategies. Excavating the silt to eliminate the source of algae nutrient proved too expensive a proposition, and they began to investigate aeration systems. They settled on a network of eleven underwater diffusers run by five compressors, installed by Aquatic Eco Systems of Apopka, Florida. Installation totaled approximately $6000, and the electrical costs are estimated at about $3500 annually, to be shared by lakeside residents. The diffusion system reduces algae without chemical sprays, ameliorates the effect of agricultural runoff, helps to renew the fish population, and quickens decomposition of the silt layer.

Trout farmers point out that diffusers tend to destratify water temperatures, which may eliminate the cool layer of water trout need in the summer. If your pond is too hot for trout, a diffuser isn't going to improve it. In fact, care should be taken during installation to ensure that the compressor is not blowing hot air into the water. The compressor can be set up in a cool, shaded area, and the line buried to help keep the air chilled.

Diffusers require maintenance to keep the venting holes clean. Depending on the size of the holes, the frequency of use, and the water conditions, slime will accumulate on the diffuser and cause back pressure on the compressor. A gauge can be installed on the compressor to monitor pressure.

Paddlewheel aeration is one of the oldest mechanical

techniques for oxygenating water, and although rather cumbersome, continues to prove popular, particularly in aquacultural setups throughout Asia. Paddlewheel aerators can be set up on floats, powered by an onboard motor, or driven by a tractor's power take-off. Oxygen levels can be boosted quickly, and circulation established, making paddlewheels especially effective at stopping fishkills.

How to Buy a Used Pond

Ponds are born, and ponds are made. A pond can form naturally in a wet hollow or it can be built by man. The advantage of a man-made pond is that you choose a site where the pond can be used conveniently. The easier it is to reach, the more likely it will be used in all the ways a pond is valuable: for recreation, irrigation, aquaculture, fire protection, and so forth. Hence the current popularity of pond building.

There is a standard operating procedure for designing and building a pond. First sort out exactly what uses the pond will fulfill. Then check the site for soil and water quality. Determine the watershed acreage. Consider the budget. That is the routine. If you attend to the steps faithfully, you'll have a good chance of building a successful pond.

Reviving an old or ailing pond is a different kettle of fish. There it sits. It may be loaded with silt or algae, or choked with weeds. It may leak. Perhaps it's empty. The pond may have been dug decades before the present owner took possession of the land, with entirely different, perhaps opposing goals in mind.

As a pond designer I enjoy the challenge of a pond revival. Inside that old pond is a new pond waiting to emerge— often in better shape than the original.

At first glance buying land with a pond seems like a good way to shortcut the effort and risk involved in building one from scratch. No preliminary siting work, no searching for the right contractor, no hassles over permits or machinery chewing up the yard. Perhaps this explains why a house with a pond often sells faster than a similar one without. A realtor told me not long ago, "A lot of people who want ponds just like to make a phone call and write a check." A lot of the same people quickly discover that buying a used pond is like buying a used car: you just bought someone else's troubles, but they're underwater.

Recently, a woman called me to report that her pond had turned into a half-acre of algae muck, and "there's a horrible smell coming up out of the water." Her family had moved into an old farmhouse the previous winter. The pond lay a couple hundred feet downhill from the house. As it turned out, the pond was choked with sediment and contaminated by runoff from an ancient septic system. Not only did the basin need dredging, but the septic system had to be relocated and rebuilt. So much for appraising a pond under a couple of feet of snow.

How to evaluate an existing pond? Begin with a walk around the edge, noting the water quality. Is it clear, cloudy, blooming with algae, infested with weeds? Is water flowing out of the pond through an outlet or spillway, or is the water static?

Clear, or even slightly cloudy water, usually indicates good water quality, while the presence of algae and weeds can spell trouble. A continuing flow of water through a pond is a good indicator of healthy oxygen levels and temperature, while stagnant water is liable to threaten fish and hasten eutrophication, the natural aging process of a pond. Of course, water quality will vary with the season, and evidence of algae during hot weather doesn't necessarily

Extensive aquatic vegetation in an older pond indicates that the basin may need to be drained and cleaned out.

mean the pond is terminal. Depending on the nature of the pond, there may be wild areas of cattails and other aquatic vegetation purposely included as protective cover and a food source for wildlife. However, extensive submerged and emergent aquatic vegetation often means the pond should be cleaned out.

Antonia Richie is a real estate broker in Woodstock, Vermont, where many properties include ponds. She observed that prospective buyers are usually repelled by algae and weeds. "People see green stuff and they get turned off," she said, "especially people who can't imagine fixing up a small problem." Conceivably a poorly maintained pond might work in the buyer's favor, as leverage to help lower the price tag. Naturally you'd want to be confident that the pond could be rejuvenated at a reasonable cost. Conversely, Richie said that a good-looking pond clearly enhances property value. "The key word is good-looking."

A pond diagnosis doesn't end with a weed survey. Leakage is often a problem. Water that drops a foot or so below overflow level during the height of summer isn't a sure sign the pond is doomed. But low water during periods of more generous precipitation hints at problems with leakage, inadequate inflow, or both.

Note whether it is an excavated or embankment pond. An excavated pond, dug into the ground with little or no dam, is less likely to give you trouble with leakage. If the pond has an embankment, check the outside slope to be sure there is no leakage. Check for signs of erosion, particularly around the overflow area. If the pond has a natural overland spillway system, the channel may need work to stabilize erosion. A piped overflow might require stabilization where water exits the outlet pipe. Check piping to be sure there are no leaks around the outside of the pipe, as well as inside, which could indicate faulty piping or leakage through the dam. Older ponds with metal outlets are particularly vulnerable to leakage due to rust.

Sometimes leaks due to porous soil can be remedied by lining the basin with clay. In extreme cases, plastic liners may be used to overcome leaks. Supplementary water also can be used to make up for losses. It's a rare pond that won't respond to some treatment, although the therapy may cost as much as the original construction. I have yet to see a frustrated owner order a pond bulldozed into oblivion. But I have heard tales.

Next, check out the shore area around the pond. The slope down into the water should be roughly 2:1 or 3:1, except perhaps in shallower beach areas. Shallow slopes are almost certain to nurture weeds and algae; excessively steep slopes can erode. It's important to know the pond depth throughout the basin. Areas shallower than four or five feet will encourage weeds and algae. Depths greater than six or seven feet are preferred. Occasionally prospective buyers interested in confirming pond depths take out a boat and use a weighted string or rod for measuring.

Inflows, particularly year-round streams running into the pond, are likely to carry in silt, reducing depth and nurturing weeds. Examine the inflow area to determine if silt removal is necessary. Springs feeding a pond from uphill areas sometimes erode shoreland. Is this a problem that may need repair? Sometimes drainage ditches and piping are necessary to correct erosion. If the pond is fed by a pipe from a nearby stream or other source, be sure the feed pool is maintained to prevent plugging. Inflows carrying in sediment can often be remedied by excavating a small silt pocket in the stream, near the pond.

Trees growing up around older ponds can threaten the integrity of an embankment, and it may be necessary to remove them. Roots boring into the dam seeking water can trigger leaks. Moreover, the closer the trees, the more leaves and needles will wind up in the water, adding to the nutrient load and potential algae problem.

The watershed that drains into the pond should be free of contaminants and nutrients, whether from livestock, septic systems, or other sources. For example, how near is the pond to public roads? It's not helpful to have road salt leaching into the basin, or debris kicked up by snowplows or road graders. Ditches, berms, or fence barriers can help deflect such roadside contamination. If you plan to raise fish, it might be wise to check the water quality with a chemical test kit to determine the pH level and oxygen saturation. Water temperature will also affect fish health.

It's helpful to know the history of a pond. I've been called in on numerous restoration projects where basin drainage was the first priority, and yet the owner couldn't recall whether the pond included a drain. In older ponds it's not unusual for sediment to cover the drainpipe at the bottom of the pond. Perhaps the owner knows there is a drain, but not what mechanism controls it. Sometimes drain plugs and caps jam and need a nudge to open up. A long pipe thrust from the outside, through the drain pipe, will often open up a stubborn cap. A firm clout with a sledgehammer helps.

Discuss the background of the pond with the owners. Knowing when the pond was built will help you determine if a cleanout is called for. It's not unusual for a pond to need a drawdown and cleaning, or complete dredging, every ten years or so. The way the pond was used will help determine what repairs or cleanouts may be needed. In all likelihood, a pond used for livestock watering will have eroded banks and a high nutrient load, which translates into repairs if the aim is to transform it into a decent swimming pond. I've seen ponds used as reflecting pools, surrounded by decorative plants and shrubs, where chemicals were used regularly to control algae. I'd be hesitant to let livestock drink from such a pond without testing the water for chemical residues. Perhaps a plastic liner or chemical sealant was used to waterproof the pond. Dredging such a pond would damage the seal.

Next, find out what variety of fish was stocked. There's no point in pouring a batch of small trout fry into a pond full of larger trout or bass; the fry will be gobbled up.

Ask how well the pond held water during dry summer months. That way you won't be surprised to find the water level dropping during a similar stretch of weather, and you'll be prepared to take corrective action, if necessary. Find out about beavers and other pond critters. If the pond has been troubled by beavers building dams or muskrats burrowing into the basin, you may have to carry on the struggle to fend them off.

The name of the pond builder can be helpful if trouble surfaces. If low water levels plague a pond, it helps to know what kind of soils are in the basin or embankment, or whether test pits were dug prior to construction. Low water levels may result from construction flaws or lack of water, or both. Knowing how the pond was built helps diagnose the problem. Was the dam built with a core trench packed with clay at the base? Was the dam foundation stripped of topsoil? If not, begin looking for the source of the leakage in the dam itself. On the other hand, a lack of test pits, or test pits dug in wet weather creating a false impression, could indicate that the pond was built without sufficient on-site water. Often the pond builder is the only one who knows these details.

What of a pond troubled by off-color, oily runoff leaching into the basin? Perhaps during construction trees were buried in the banks around the pond and are now decaying, producing the seepage. Was there an old shop, garage, or source of chemicals upstream? A barn? These could be the source of contaminants or nutrients troubling the pond. The better you know a pond's history, the better you can care for it.

For your own peace of mind, it's reassuring to know that a pond can supply the water needed to extinguish a fire, particularly if a hydrant has been installed. Moreover, depending on where you live, fire insurance premiums may be discounted because of a pond. Be sure hydrant inlets have not silted over.

Finally, it's important to mesh a pond's natural attributes with your plans for use. Consider how you plan to use the pond, and measure the pond's corresponding qualifications. A small pond might be fine for agricultural irrigation but, because of dramatic drops in the water level during pumping, be a poor medium for raising fish. Conversely, a pond set up for fish culture may not have enough surplus water to supply irrigation or hydro needs. A pond used to raise waterfowl may not be very appetizing for swimmers. Often, however, a pond can serve many overlapping functions simultaneously. A general-purpose recreation pond is usually fine for swimming, skating, backyard garden irrigation, and raising some fish, along with the capacity to attract wildlife and afford fire protection.

Aside from conforming to good construction and aquaculture standards, pond appearance is really a matter of taste. Landscaping options range from a hands-off wild look to elaborate floral plantings, fountains, and pink flamingos. Location is one thing you can't change, but don't let anyone tell you that the best pond must lie in full view of the house. Indeed, a living room view of your own private waterfront has a magical ambience, but a pond set back in the woods has another charm. It magnetizes animals that might be timid about appearing near a human habitat. A friend of mine recalls an Indian summer day she spent swimming and relaxing beside her secluded pond. As she sat on the bank, a buck crashed out of the woods, leapt into the pond, and swam across. He stepped out on the other side, shook himself off, and kept running. Close encounters like that are worth a hike through the brush.

Appendix
Pond Culture Resources

Please consult Books in Print, your local Cooperative Extension Service, the Soil Conservation Service, or the US Government Printing Office for current availability of books, pamphlets and brochures.

BOOKS

Axelrod, Herbert. *Koi of the World: Japanese Colored Carp.* T.F.H. Publications, 211 West Sylvia Ave., P.O. Box 27, Neptune City, NJ 07753

Bardach, John E. *Aquaculture: The Farming and Husbandry of Freshwater & Marine Organisms.* John Wiley & Sons, Inc., 605 Third Ave., New York, NY 10016

Bennett, George W. *Management of Lakes and Ponds.* Van Nostrand Reinhold Company, 135 West 50th St., New York, NY 10020

Brown, E. Evan. *World Fish Farming: Cultivation and Economics.* Avi Publishing Company, Westport, CT 06880

Curtis, Brian. *The Life Story of the Fish.* Dover Publications, Inc., 11 East Second St., Mineola, NY 11501

Edwards, David J. *Salmon and Trout Farming in Norway.* Fishing News Books LTD, One Long Garden Walk, Farnham, Surrey, England

Kabish, Klaus and Joachim Hammerling. *Ponds and Pools—Oases in the Landscape.* Arco Publishing, Inc., 215 Park Ave. South, New York, NY 10003

Limburg, Peter. *Farming the Waters.* Beaufort Books, 9 East 40th St., New York, NY 10016

Reid, George K. *Pond Life.* Golden Guide Series, Western Publishing Company, Inc., 1220 Mound Ave., Racine, WI 53404

Russell, Franklin. *Watchers at the Pond.* Time Reading Program, Time, Inc., Rockefeller Center, New York, NY 10020

Sedgwick, S. Dummond. *Trout Farming Handbook.* Scholium International, Inc., 130-30 31st Ave., Flushing, NY 11354

Walton, Isaak. *The Compleat Angler.* E.P. Dutton, 2 Park Ave., New York, NY 10016

US Department of Agriculture Soil Conservation Service. *Ponds—Planning, Design, Construction.* Handbook Number 590, US Government Printing Office, Washington, DC 20402

PAMPHLETS

Aquaculture Development Program of the Department of Land & Natural Resources. *Aquaculture in Hawaii Newsletter.* Room 359, 355 Merchant St., Honolulu, HI 96813

Garden Way Publishing. *Building a Pond for Food and Fun.* Garden Way Bulletin A-19. Garden Way Publishing, Schoolhouse Road, Pownal, VT 05261

Submatic Irrigation Systems, *Submatic Drip Irrigation Catalog.* P.O. Box 246, Lubbock, TX 79408

Vermont Cooperative Extension Service. *Fish Farming in Vermont.* University of Vermont, 601 Main St., Burlington, VT 05401

MAGAZINES

Aquaculture Magazine. (Bimonthly with Annual Buyer's Guide). Box 2329, Asheville, NC 28802

Canadian Aquaculture. (Five issues per year with Annual Buyer's Guide). 4611 William Head Rd., Victoria, BC V8X 3W9

Farm Pond Harvest Magazine. (Four issues per year). R.R. 3, Box 197, Momence, IL 60954

MAPS

Raised Relief Topographic Maps
TSI Supply, P.O. Box 151, Flanders, NJ 07836
Write for index map

United States Geographical Survey Maps,
Map Distribution Branch
Box 25286, Denver Federal Center, Denver, CO 80225

ORGANIZATIONS

California Aquaculture Association
P.O. Box 1004, Niland, CA 92257
Newsletter, *California Aquatic Farming*

The New Alchemy Institute
237 Hatchville Rd., East Falmouth, MA 02536
Newsletters, books, and workshops on small-scale aquaculture and farming.

U.S. Trout Farmer's Association
P.O. Box 220, Harper's Ferry, WV 26525
Magazine, *Salmonid*, on the trout industry

EQUIPMENT/MANAGEMENT

FISHING SUPPLIES AND POND MANAGEMENT

Aquatic Eco-Systems, Inc., Box 1446, Apopka, FL 32704

Aquaculture Research Environmental Associates, P.O. Box 1303, Homestead, FL 33090 (305-248-4205)

Aquatic Control, Inc., P.O. Box 100, Seymour, IN 47274 (812-497-2410)

DM&J Aquatic Weed Control, Box 294, Hebron, IL 60034 (815-648-4083)

Memphis Net & Twine, 2481 Matthews Ave., P.O. Box 8331, Memphis, TN 38108 (901-458-2656/800-238-6380)

Nichols Net & Twine, Rt. 3, Bend Road, East St. Louis, IL 62201 (618-876-7700)

Staff Industries, Inc. (pond liners), 240 Chene St., Detroit, MI 48207 (800-526-1368)

Tetra Liners (pond liners), Warner Lambert, 201 Tabor Rd., Morris Plains, NJ 07950

Eager, Inc., 526 North 700 West, P.O. Box 476, North Salt Lake, UT 84054

AquaShade, Inc., P.O. Box 198, Eldred, NY 12732

Aquabacta Aid, Water Quality Science, Inc. P.O. Box 532, Bolivar, MO 65613

Water Test Kits—Ammonia, Carbon Dioxide, Dissolved Oxygen, pH, and Water Hardness

Hatch Chemical Company, P.O. Box 907, Ames, IA 50010

Water Circulators and Aerators

Aeration Industries International, Inc., P.O. Box 59144, Minneapolis, MN 55459 (612-448-6789)

Air-O-Lator Corp., 8100 Paslo, Kansas City, MO 64131

Barebo, Inc., Otterbine Aerators, P.O. Box 217, RD 2, Emmaus, PA 18049

Fresh Flo Corporation (fresh flo aerators), Rt. 1, Highway 28 SW, Cascade, WI 53011 (414-528-8236)

Grovehac, Inc., 4310 N. 126th St., Brookfield, WI 53005 (414-781-5020)

Lake Aid Systems (wind-powered water circulator), Box 1262, Bismarck, ND 58501 (701-738-1355)

Pond Landscaping
Lilypons Water Gardens, Lilypons, MD 21717

Paradise Water Gardens, 14 May St., Whitman, MA 02382

Van Ness Water Gardens, 2460 N. Euclid Ave., Upland, CA 91786-1199

William Tricker, Inc., 7125 Tanglewood Dr., Independence, OH 44131

Wildlife Ponds
Environmental Concern, Inc., P.O. Box P, 210 W. Chew Ave, St. Michaels, MD 21663

Kester's Wild Game Food Nursery, P.O. Box 516, Omro, WI 54963

Wildlife Nurseries, P.O. Box 2724, Oshkosh, WI 54903

FISH

Trout

Brown's Trout Hatchery, RT 362, Bliss, NY 14024 (716-322-7322)

Cedar Springs Trout Hatchery, RT 2, Mill Hall, PA (717-726-3737)

Fernwood Limne, Inc., Fish and Consulting Services, 77 RT 9, Gansevoort, NY 12831 (518-793-1282)

Great Brook Trout Farm, RD 1, Plainfield, VT 05667 (802-454-7721)

Hy-On-A Hill Trout Hatchery, Box 308, Plainfield, NH 03781 (603-675-6267)

Imlay City Fish Farm, 1442 N. Summers Road, Imlay City, MI 48444 (313-724-2185)

Jan L. Michalek, 11830 Camp Ohio Road, NE, St. Louisville, OH 43071 (614-745-2187)

Mt. Lassen Trout Farm, Route 5, Box 36, Red Bluff, CA 96080 (916-597-2222)

Waterland, Corp., Route 242, Mountain Road, Montgomery Center, VT 05471 (802-326-4215)

Warm Water Fish—Bass, Bluegills, Common Carp, Channel Catfish, Hybrid Sunfish

John B. Fitzpatrick Fishery Management Service, 214 East North Street, Dwight, IL 6020 (815-584-2545)

Opel's Fish Hatchery, RR1, Box 51, Worden, IL 62097 (618-459-3287)

Zetts Fish Farm and Hatchery, Drifting, PA 16834

Triploid Grass Carp, White Amur, Bighead

Malone's Fish Farm, Highway 31 South, P.O. Box 158, Lonoke, AR 72086 (501-676-2800)

Index